Building Peace

Building Peace
Overcoming Violence in Communities

Mary Yoder Holsopple, Ruth E. Krall
and Sharon Weaver Pittman

WCC Publications, Geneva

Cover design: Marie Arnaud Snakkers
Cover photo: Ecumenical Accompaniment
Programme in Palestine and Israel (EAPPI)

ISBN 2-8254-1426-3

© 2004 WCC Publications
World Council of Churches
150 route de Ferney, P.O. Box 2100
1211 Geneva 2, Switzerland
Web site: http://www.wcc-coe.org

No. 108 in the Risk Book Series

Printed in Switzerland

Table of Contents

1	FOREWORD *Fernando Enns*
4	PROLOGUE
16	1. WHAT ARE WE TALKING ABOUT?
28	2. EDUCATION: TEACHING A CULTURE OF PEACE
46	3. THE HEALTH SECTOR: A FRONT-LINE FOR BUILDING PEACE
59	4. THE RELIGIOUS SECTOR: MORAL COMPASS FOR PEACE-BUILDING
74	5. THE MEDIA: MESSAGE BEARERS FOR PEACE-BUILDING
83	6. COMMUNITY ORGANIZATIONS AND THE PUBLIC SECTOR
94	7. IF YOU WANT PEACE, WORK FOR JUSTICE
105	APPENDIX: VIOLENCE PREVENTION SPECTRUM
106	REFERENCES

Foreword

"It takes a village to raise a child." The pure and simple wisdom of this African proverb is the basis of proactive peace-making, of building a culture of peace.

We experience cultures of violence in every sphere of life. If we define culture as the sum of all created forms of human expression and language, of all orders and institutions of communities, their moral standards as well as their interpretations and visions of reality, then it becomes clear that a holistic approach is needed to change the existing culture of violence into a culture of peace.

The ecumenical "*Decade to Overcome Violence 2001-2010:* Churches Seeking Reconciliation and Peace", initiated by the World Council of Churches, is following this ambitious approach. It calls churches, ecumenical organizations and all people of good will to work together for peace, justice and reconciliation at all levels – local, regional and global. This is a call to interact and collaborate with local communities, secular movements and people of other living faiths in order to cultivate a culture of peace. This includes a summons to repentance: "We must begin with ourselves, with the ways we think and the ways we act in our families, our neighbourhoods, our countries and our churches." Delegates of churches around the globe established the Decade, as a means to overcome the spirit, logic and practice of violence. This includes the effort to overcome theological justifications of violence, to affirm anew the spirituality of reconciliation and active nonviolence. We want to be and build healing communities of peace in diversity, founded on truth and embracing creative approaches to peace-building. In order to succeed, strong alliances are needed among individuals, communities, networks and movements working towards a culture of peace.

The ecumenical decade was launched in conjunction with the United Nations initiative that proclaimed the years 2001-2010 the "*International Decade for a Culture of Peace and Non-Violence for the Children of the World*". In the midst of a proliferation of regional, local, ethnic, religious and civil conflicts and terrorism around the world, this initiative also emphasizes the need for a global transition from a culture of war to a culture of peace. The mandate for the Decade specifically emphasizes "the need for the international community to recognize and implement strategies to focus on and ensure assistance for children exposed to harmful and violent situations".

This book is precisely the contribution that is needed for these initiatives. It marks a major shift from individual action to community action, from healing to prevention, from being reactive to becoming proactive. For it is not enough to be in solidarity with the victims of violence, it is not enough to create homeless shelters, soup kitchens and centres for the healing of trauma. In order to change a culture, it is necessary to analyze and wrestle with the root causes of violence.

The strong motivation of the authors arises from experience as well as academic reflection. These three women have been trained in various disciplines and are gifted in encouraging others to become active contributors to a peace-filled culture. They promote the fullness of life for all. They are mothers, social workers, social scientists, teachers, psychiatric nurses, academics and theologians. They have experienced terrible violence in various contexts from Mozambique to Kosovo, from Central America to Iraq and within the US. Out of these experiences they provide examples for building peace. While confronted with the typical "dilemma of the healer", they carry within themselves a healthy commitment to relentless analysis of the causes of the disease. Through this process they have become prophetic voices for the creation of a society that encourages fullness of life for all.

In order to understand the complexities of violence as well as proactive peace-building, an interdisciplinary approach is indispensable. Collecting the wisdom of peace-builders from many regions and backgrounds, the authors invite us to become part of their journey of encouragement and empowerment. Everyone is needed, every member of the community can play a role in this endeavour. The concrete examples provided by the authors can be applied to many different cultural contexts. Their book is a strong and convincing invitation to leave the status of bystanders behind and become peace-builders. It moves from theory to practical guidance and specific instructions for building alternatives to society as we know it.

This book offers more than a call to become part of the movement for a culture of peace. It presents concrete steps and programmes for the prevention of violence. Individuals and communities are discovering the spirituality of nonviolence, the art of healing as well as the power and promise of reconciliation. Restoration of relations is the key element for building a culture of peace. In this restoration process, religion is indispensable to instil values of caring and healing because through faith we know ourselves to have been reconciled and healed by the grace of God – and therefore empowered to live in peace as ambassadors of reconciliation.

May this book become an inspiration to all those who do not believe that it is possible to change the world, as well as to those who already "have a dream" that one day violence shall be overcome.

Fernando Enns
Heidelberg University, Germany

Prologue

The three authors, all from the USA, come to the writing of this book with widely disparate, yet rich, life experiences. Ruth has recently retired as professor of religion and psychology at Goshen College, a Mennonite institution in northern Indiana, chairing the peace, justice and conflict studies programme for 18 years. Sharon retired as chair of the social work department at Andrews University, an Adventist institution in southwestern Michigan and is now assisting in the re-establishment of health care in Iraq. Mary was director of the Peace and Justice Collaborative, an effort of Andrews University, Associated Mennonite Biblical Seminary and Goshen College at the beginning of this project, and she is now a social worker in an inner city elementary school in northern Indiana. We have work experience in theology, nursing, social work, counselling and international development. It is from this experience that we write a book that combines community development and public health paradigms in an effort to reduce violence and build peace in local communities. We thought it would be helpful to begin with three self-introductions sketching our personal backgrounds and ideas for creating a culture of peace.

Mary Yoder Holsopple

In the hot, dusty, low veldt of Swaziland I experienced first-hand what it means to live the precarious life of a refugee. White tents, turned brown from the wind-swept dust, row upon row, with only an occasional tree to provide shade, housed 25,000 refugees from Mozambique. People carried on with the basics of living – searching for food and firewood, water and clothing. Sporadic pit latrines provided sanitation. School children gathered in whatever shade could be found to listen to a teacher give a lesson without supplies, books, other supplies or even a building to house them. A hastily built health clinic provided health care, with clinicians doing their best to care for the children who frequently experienced dysentery due to the crowded conditions.

While it was important to provide relief goods in the form of food, clothing, blankets, towels, health and school supplies, I came to realize that my contribution was barely keeping the people alive on minimum calorie requirements calculated when we distributed food relief. Yes, we were keeping them alive, but were we providing enough nutrition and protein to help the brains of the children develop and reach their full potential?

I watched as the refugees dropped to their knees to pick up the last kernels of maize that fell from the trucks and bags during the delivery and distribution. I saw people fighting over rations to make sure they received their fair portion. Their ration had to feed their family for a month. If it fell short, it would not last and they would be hungry. Who would go without food so that others could live? The refugees faced such decisions daily.

Reality hit me forcefully. It obliged me to ask: Can we put as many resources into stopping the war that creates the refugee situation as we put into providing relief supplies? It takes massive amounts of energy, time and money to provide goods for relief. I know because that is what I did for five years. Can we devote at least the same amount of resources to bring the war to an end? Or, even better, can we work more proactively at preventing wars from happening in the first place?

After the war ended in Mozambique, it became clear to me and my Mozambican colleagues in a local non-governmental organization: there were far more resources available from well-meaning groups in wealthy nations to provide reactive relief efforts during a time of crisis than there were for proactive development efforts to prevent catastrophes like wars from happening. In other words, the message seems to be, "If you are killing each other, we can provide money and other goods to assist in your need. If you want to build schools and health clinics to help the populace and prevent war, we do not have resources for that."

Fast-forward a few years. I found myself in a middle school in a Midwestern town in the United States. As the social worker, I worked with youth from all walks of life. I provided a food basket and moral support to Steven and his family who were living in their car, surrounded on all sides by affluence and abundance. They could not stay in the homeless shelter because they were unwilling to give up the family pet, having given up every other possession. The pet provided consistent, loving comfort. This family was experiencing the violence of poverty.

I also worked with Linda who was bright but confused. Her sixteen-year-old brother was incarcerated for dealing drugs. Her father wanted nothing to do with her, having thrown her and a few possessions out of his house. Her mother had a health condition that prevented her from working and caused depression. While this young woman was bright, she often skipped school and rarely performed to her ability when she was in school. Her choices continually put her in situations of violence as she suffered emotional, physical and sexual abuse.

I will never forget the day she sat in my office sobbing. Through tears she eloquently stated her dilemma: "Mrs. Holsopple, everyone is telling me I have to get out of the gang. My probation officer, my counsellor, you – everyone tells me the gang is no good for me and that I need to get out. How can I do that? They are the only family I know. They are the people who love me and who will always be there for me."

What could I say? She was right. People attempting to help her came and went from her life. How many counsellors, social workers and case managers had she had in her young life? And where were they now? This young woman had been an active gang member for two years. She was twelve years old.

What leads a ten-year-old girl to join a street gang? What makes a family flee a war, only to become refugees? Why is a young boy living in a car while surrounded by affluence? Although these situations seem worlds apart, they share elements in common. One is desperation: a basic need to survive. Our children are living amidst the violence of poverty, the violence of domestic squabbles and sexual assault, the violence of war.

And what is our response? We give them just enough to keep them alive, but not enough to help them thrive and enjoy life to its fullest.

I have been fortunate. By accident of birth, I have a loving family. I received a good education. I have been able to travel and work in a variety of settings. I have learned about community development, about the wonder of empowering people to help themselves. I have learned about the saving power of public health – of clean water supplies and good sanitation. I have learned about the resiliency of people. I have been humbled by what those whom society sees as being the poorest of the poor have taught me.

In my wandering, I have wondered about how proactive peace-building can eliminate the need to assist refugees and prevent ten-year-old girls from affiliating with gangs. What do we need to do differently?

Out of this wandering and wondering, I set out on a quest to see what communities are doing to prevent violence and build peace. What I found was a cadre of good people doing great things, using a variety of theories and paradigms. In this book, I bring together some of those basic themes in an attempt to articulate a way to work proactively at the issues that our communities and nations face. I hold on to the belief that if we truly wanted to, we could lessen the severity of poverty and diffuse conflicts before they become wars.

That is the premise of this book. It presents community development theory with a public health focus. It highlights the role of resiliency and shows that collaborative effort, utilizing a prevention spectrum, can contribute to community peace. But it goes beyond that to promote a strengths-based paradigm that can build peace in our neighbourhoods, wherever we may find ourselves.

Sharon Weaver Pittman

I am writing this foreword from Iraq. The human toll from years of violence is evident each day in my work here. I am awed by the power and resiliency of Iraqi people to overcome violence with activities that support peace-building.

They inspire me daily to share their strategies and document their efforts at building a peace-filled community.

My personal motivations and beliefs are crafted by my life experience. As with many who are blessed with education and family support, I have lived a privileged life. I grew up in Karachi, Pakistan, where my parents gave me the advantage of living in an environment of diversity in ethnicity, religion and culture. My American roots and our governmental motives, however, were constantly challenged as "imperialistic" and "evil". While I lived among the constant rhetoric of "jihad" from the few, I also learned that the majority of people were wonderful, caring and kind, and over the years of living among them they became my extended family.

As an adult, my life as a social worker kept me constantly facing the impact of violence and its ability to destroy the human spirit. Each day the emergency room of the hospital where I worked was full of victims of violence. Rape and child abuse were daily occurrences that could have made me numb if I had approached my work only as a clinician. But I cannot distance myself from the pain of human brutality and remain a dynamic and passionate advocate for the powerless and victimized.

* * *

I listened as Debbie screamed: "If I find him, I'll kill him. All I wanted was just to take a few minutes to have a quiet lunch in the park!" It was a beautiful fall day in a small town in southeastern Washington state, and Debbie, a busy mother of four, had decided to take a few minutes to enjoy her lunch in a park. Her quiet lunch became a nightmare when she was pulled into a nearby pick-up truck and brutally raped. That day, Debbie's family lost their sense of safety and well-being to the brutal effects of violence. And all I could do was listen.

Beyond the trauma of violence I have experienced in emergency rooms and my counselling office, I have lived the impact of violence on children around the world. From the four Guatemalan sons I adopted after the violent death of their father and their mother's inability to feed them, to the victims of war with whom I work in my emergency response and international relief work, the price of violence motivates me to work at peace and safety-enhancing activities.

My life, like the lives of all who embrace the spectrum of human experience, has been shaped in part by the power of tears. I have dried the tears of Kosovar refugee children in camps in Albania, fresh from the horrors of violence that they experienced. Little Rafee, with his tear-stained face, described to me how he had just spent two nights tied to the body of his dead uncle, left there by the same soldiers he watched kill his father. Rafee had lost his childhood innocence to political and tribal hatred.

Why am I inspired to write a book on preventing violence and building peace? Because the voices and the tears of those who have suffered the brutality of violence demand that I advocate for civility and community well-being in addition to promoting responsible and proactive approaches to peace-building. The passion of my convictions motivates me to emphasize a practical rather than theoretical approach to peace-building. Together with my co-authors, I have chosen not to discuss the problem of violence in the abstract. Our personal and professional lives have allowed us to experience worlds of violence. This book is an opportunity to bring together the wisdom of peace-builders from many regions to share their success stories with you. As social scientists we are aware that peace-building is far from a simple activity. We know that the best models, having the greatest impact, are those through which an entire community is involved in building a violence-free society. Our hope is that any group of motivated peace-builders will be able to use this manual to glean ideas that can be culturally adapted and applied to a local setting. We also know that to build a world of peace will take a lot of creativity. We hope that you will become partners sharing your ideas and best practices so that we may work together to craft a world where our children and grandchildren can thrive in peace and safety.

Ruth E. Krall

My thinking about violence has been shaped by my religious faith, and my religious faith has been shaped by my encounters with violence. Forbidden by my Mennonite mother to play with guns in childhood, nevertheless I took every opportunity I could find to play with my childhood friend's toy guns and other weaponry. I understood the joy of discovering exactly how cap pistols and water pistols could be used in play with other children. The underlying parental message, however, came though loud and clear. Playing with guns at make-believe killing was not acceptable behaviour for children because violence was not appropriate behaviour for adults.

As I reflect on my own personal interests in creating a different path to solving intense and deeply felt conflicts, I am aware of several crucial crossroads where I have had to choose what I believed and what I did.

As a psychiatric nurse clinician in my 20s, I saw the consequences of violence played out in the lives of real people. Part of my graduate preparation included two years of clinical work in a United States Veterans Hospital. These former soldiers from the first and second world wars and from the Korean conflict of the 1950s were men who suffered. Here I first heard about the clinical diagnosis of "shell shock." Yet no one mentioned their participation in war and killing as one of the roots of their suffering. Instead, usually it was assumed that each man's suffering was due to his own personal weakness.

By the time I began, much later in time, to meet in a clinical setting the returned veterans of the Vietnam war (men who had been captured and imprisoned by the Viet Cong), my questions about war had become clearer. Because of my place in the generation that had protested this war, I understood that the trauma of killing and the trauma of being hunted and killed were related if not identical.

Much later I would read the Vietnamese Buddhist monk Thich Nhat Hanh and discover his concept of "interbeing". In Nhat Hanh's thinking, we are all interconnected because we are living, conscious human beings. The sufferings of one are the sufferings of us all. As a result of reading Nhat Hanh, I came to understand that even as an unwilling witness to the killing done in warfare, I also could have been the killer or the killed. An accident of national and class privilege at birth was all that separated me from the brutal killing fields in which, as the American poet Maya Angelou so eloquently has put it, "millions of ourselves have killed millions of ourselves".

There is an apocryphal story that periodically resurfaces in American medical, nursing and public health journals. In that narrative, two individuals are walking downstream below a swiftly falling waterfall. They hear the screams of a small child who is in the water. They dive into the river and save the child. As they continue walking down the river, more children are screaming for help. Each time the couple dive into the river and rescue the children. However, after a period of this continuous diving and rescuing, one of the two turns around and begins to run upstream. His companion calls, "Hey! You can't leave me here alone! We must keep rescuing these children!" The runner pauses, turns around and calls back, "I am going upstream to see who is throwing the children into this river, and I am going to stop them."

This is the dilemma of the healer. There are more than enough victims of violence to occupy a life-time of clinical work.

Another path in my personal journey was bifurcated in time. As a high school student, I came to understand that American practices of racism were violent. I decided to learn about changing my own behaviour so that I could establish friendships that were not confined within one skin colour or one ethnic group. As did many others in my generation, I began to join in the marches that protested American apartheid.

Later, much later, I came to understand that sexism was a structure in which my own life was limited. I began to realize the infrastructure of oppression. I began to understand the role of systemic injustice in the perpetuation of violence and oppression. I wrote my doctoral dissertation on rape's effects on the lives of young women. For the first time, as my own experience in the world, I began to understand rage. I began to understand hatred. I began to understand violence. As a woman, studying the results of sexual violation in the lives of other women, I began to understand fear.

I turned, for a short while, from my companions who were downstream rescuing women. I ran upstream into theological studies to see what was happening closer to the source that allowed people to do such violence against other people. What I found, in looking at Western and American culture, was a common and popular culture that sanctioned violence and promoted it as the way to solve problems in human and national relationships. Popular cultural violence was, I found, securely anchored in the long history of Christendom in the West.

While the violence of rape and the violence of war have many distinguishing characteristics, I found that they have much more in common. The suffering of the victims was a common, soundless cry for justice as well as for human compassion and understanding.

The training of my childhood helped me to make connections. What we learn by modelling and active teaching is what we will become. Unless there is an accessible alternative model for our lives, in our own bodies and psyches, we become the bridge from past to future over which violence will walk to perpetuate itself.

I began the spiritual discipline of seeking to change my own Americanized spirit of violence. I actively hunted for the voices of individuals in the world who were making a difference – who were seeking solutions to the perplexing questions of violence in human life. In the great religious wisdom traditions of the world, I found profound 20th-century avatars of peace: Mahatma Gandhi, Martin Luther King, Jr, Julia Esquivel, Thomas Merton, Fanny Lou Hamer, Nelson Mandela, Joanna Rogers Macy, Mother Teresa, Cesar Chavez, the Berrigan Brothers, Nelle Morton, Archbishop Desmond Tutu, Thich Nhat Hanh, Dorothy Day, Howard

Thurman, Oscar Romero, A.J. Muste, Elise Boulding and Barbara Deming.

In the lives and writings of these individuals and others, I found a pervasive central concern for developing the individual's inner spirit as one of peace in place of contentiousness. Fighting for peace made no sense. Aggressiveness in pursuing justice often meant that the peace-building movement itself did violence to those who disagreed with a particular ideological form of peace work in the world. Rather, these avatars urged their readers and students to recognize that we ourselves need, in each moment, to become the peace. In our thoughts as well as in our actions, it was important to come to a central place of balance and harmony so that our strong, focused actions on behalf of peace emerged from this place of joy, balance, contentment and harmony rather than from rage, anger, hatred, distrust and discontent.

Having earlier witnessed the utter devastation of war zones and rape zones, and the lengthy process of healing needed by warriors and perpetrators as well as by victims of violence, I returned to my role as healer more committed to seeking ways we could prevent the trauma of victimization, ways we could lessen or prevent the violence we human beings are all too willing to direct towards the lives and cultures of others.

I am passionate about the belief that many aspects of peace-building are necessary. We must not only stop or lessen violence that has begun; we must work to prevent it from happening in the first place. We must seek not only to heal the wounds that live on inside individuals and their communities; we must seek to find alternative ways of relating to each other. Not only must we seek to find pathways into reconciliation and forgiveness after events of violence have destroyed lives and trust, we must also create stepping stones to understanding and celebrating the blessings of human diversity. We must not only accompany victims of violence, we must also seek to recognize that we are related to its perpetrators through our common humanity. We must not only bear a sorrowful witness to that violence we cannot yet stop, we must seek ways to shout for joy and dance in the streets of our communities when peaceful solutions to complex situations of human conflict are created and become manifest among us.

Our world's children are so often taught by words and example that violence is an inevitable aspect of human interaction and human life. This theology of human fallenness must be countered with solid theological teaching that all of earth's human beings are created in the divine image. None can be sacrificed without great losses to the divine Spirit that resides within each one of us. We must believe this; we must live it; we must also teach it to children.

One of the most profound tasks for the peace-building movement of the future will be to re-examine all our human theologies in light of the question of violence. It will take courage and much faith for us to renounce beloved theologies that lead us to do so much violence to each other inside the global community. Until we are willing to do this work in many of our religious communities, however, we will not completely address the issue of prevention. Until the worldview of violence changes and we stop being the bridges across which violence marches to perpetuate itself in new generations, we will continue to know violence as our human heritage.

I believe we can – and must – evolve a new religious and spiritual consciousness in which violence becomes unacceptable as a way to solve human problems. It is not the gods who have made us violent. It is our beliefs about the gods.

From all three of us

We are writing this book for people who want to create a culture of peace in their own settings. Our intention is to provide ideas that are practical and possible. Examples of that which is working appear throughout the book. Ideas for how you can build peace in your community abound. Many of the examples come from northern Indiana and southwest Michigan. This is where we live and work, and therefore this is what we know best. You may find good examples in your community, as well. Our suggestion is that if you find something that is working well, do more of it! May you, too, find the peace that comes from working proactively towards building a better world.

* * *

We could not have written this book without the assistance of many peace-loving people. Judith Davis made magic with her editorial skills, creating one voice out of three. Larry Cohen provided the impetus with his Prevention Spectrum and gave generously of his time and encouraging comments by reading the manuscript draft. D.J. McFadden offered his expertise in public health. The Teagle Foundation offered financial support for the research and writing of this book. To them we extend sincere gratitude. We are grateful to the academic institutions with which we are affiliated – Andrews University, Associated Mennonite Biblical Seminary and Goshen College – for providing the setting for creative pondering. David Fast and Melanie Neufeld, Peace and Justice Collaborative staff, offered moral support and creative assistance – more than they will ever know! Anna Liechty Sawastsky provided invaluable research assistance. Loren Johns, Rebecca Horst, Anna, Melanie and David read the first draft and offered extremely valuable suggestions. Fernando Enns read a draft and suggested its potential value to the World Council of Churches programme, the Decade to Overcome Violence. Thank you, Fernando! To the host of people with whom we met during the research for this book and through the course of our lives – your inspiration is reflected between the covers of this book!

To our significant others, we say a sincere thank you for your love and support. Most especially to Elroy, Zebulon and Asha, whose love and encouragement kept Mary sane during the editing process, our love and gratefulness is extended.

This book is dedicated to all the children of the world. May you know and live in peace.

All names that appear in this book have been changed to protect the identities of those involved.

1. What Are We Talking About?

We live in a culture of violence. This reality hit me full force when I (Mary) returned to the United States after living in Africa for seven years. Having lived in two different war zones, I thought I was returning to a safe and tranquil setting. I was appalled by what I found in my own culture. Violent images appeared everywhere. Television, movies, video games and computer games showed scenes of violence, some of it extreme. Magazines and newspapers were filled with news of violence in our community and country.

Neither was I prepared for the *meanness* I found in my own culture. We act in cruel ways. We say things that dehumanize. We are selfish and greedy, frequently suing each other over petty grievances. We are extremely competitive. What a shock!

An even greater shock came when I remarked to my friends on the violence and meanness. Well-educated people looked at me with quizzical faces and said, "What do you mean?"

I am a mother. I want my children to grow up in a community where they feel safe going to school and walking in their neighbourhood. I want them to live in a culture of peace, in a place where the motto is, "What's good for you is also good for me." I do not want to feel compelled to teach my children what to do when (not if) the shooting starts at school.

Out of my life experience comes my passion to work at building peace in my community. I need to work at social changes that create a culture of peace. Because of my peace-church heritage and convictions, I believe that our violence reduction and prevention efforts must be carried out in peaceful ways. But I cannot do this work alone — it is essential to have the support of a community of committed, peace-loving individuals.

The world recently watched war unfold in Iraq as the United States attempted to secure itself against terrorism. In many other countries of the world, civil wars divide citizens into violent, partisan groups. In addition to war, many developing and industrialized countries experience criminal violence. In addition, structural violence continues to devastate the lives of many individuals throughout the world.

World religious leaders and spiritual teachers from many faith traditions have begun to consider the religious and spiritual implications of violence in the world community. For example, the World Council of Churches in Geneva has proclaimed the years 2001-2010 as the Decade to Overcome Violence. Churches are actively seeking peace and reconciliation, inviting all people of good will to promote efforts to overcome violence in their settings. The United Nations has declared a Decade for a Culture of Peace and Non-Violence for the Children of the World, also 2001-2010. They invite non-governmental organizations, religious and educational institutions, artists and the media to promote the Decade for the well-being of all the children of the world.

As the authors of this book discussed our individual and common understandings of violence and useful approaches for working towards a decrease in violence, we debated preventive measures. We discussed the task of healing the victims of violence. We described our individual concepts of how we could replace a culture of violence with a culture of peace, and how that culture might look in the 21st century.

To overcome violence and foster peace in the world, we decided that we must begin at home, choosing to focus this book on building peace in our own communities. Although reducing violence is a necessary component of peace-building work, it is urgent, in our opinion, to begin thinking about positive peace-building. To do this, we need to understand the stark reality of many of our communities where violence is an everyday occurrence for many of our citizens. In this book, we are committed to moving beyond the demographics and description problems. We do not intend to highlight the problems in our communities and in our world, for they are all too apparent. Rather, we intend to look at ways of building a culture of peace by enhancing our community strengths and building on those things that are already in place to promote human dignity and peace for all. It is urgent that members of our communities begin to dream and create a vision of a culture of peace. Only when we can dream and envision living in peace can we begin to create a more peaceful and less violent world for ourselves and for our children.

It is important to share a common vocabulary while thinking about and engaging in peace-building. In this chapter, we present working definitions of violence, peace, public health and community development.

The vocabulary of violence

The World Health Organization defines violence in the following way:

> The intentional use of physical force or power, threatened or actual, against oneself, another person, or against a group or community, that either results in or has a high likelihood of resulting in injury, death, psychological harm, maldevelopment or deprivation.

While most violence is recognizable, some violence is subtle and may be visible only to its victims. The late Presbyterian theologian Robert McAfee Brown has created a typology of violence. He noted that overt violence such as murder, war or terrorism is visible and easily recognized. Overt violence can occur between individuals – spouse battering or murder, for example. Or it can be legitimated within political systems, as in cases of invoking the death penalty or waging war.

Covert violence is less recognizable. Verbal abuse or emotional neglect of a child serve as examples. Other politically legitimated examples of covert violence within the socio-political arena include racist or sexist laws and social policies that eliminate equal employment opportunities. One form of covert violence is structural. Sometimes called systemic or institutionalized violence, this form of violence occurs when all (or even most) of a society's formal and informal structures create an organization of wealth and power in which individuals, sub-groups or entire communities are exploited by the structures themselves. Poverty may be seen to be one pervasive form of structural violence when the wealth of the few is created on the backs of the poor.

Conversely stated, the poverty of the many is guaranteed by the wealth of the few. While a small number of the world's families control vast sums of land and capital, millions more live in poverty so severe that they have no possibility of bettering their lives or those of their children. They are born into poverty, and they die in poverty.

Structural violence is often the most difficult form of violence to identify, assess and remedy. However, its victims know its bondage. When the powerful refuse to include the weak as full participants in a society, the resulting repression and oppression create situations in which violence breeds. Brown observes that "structural violence usually has the effect of denying people important rights, such as economic well-being; social, political and sexual equality; a sense of personal fulfilment, and self-worth".

Once we begin to understand that preventable starvation is a form of violence, that death from treatable diseases is a form of violence, that sub-standard housing that does not adequately protect families from environmental and climate hazards is a form of violence, that the inability to educate oneself or one's children is a form of violence – then we can also begin to understand the magnitude of the challenge faced in the deceptively simple concept of preventing violence and promoting peace. Even so, we firmly believe that a group of committed, peace-loving people can effect change and build a culture of peace.

The vocabulary of peace

The concept of peace is as complex as that of violence and equally difficult to define. The American Heritage Dictionary defines peace as the absence of war or hostilities. Another definition might be a freedom from quarrels or hostilities. Perhaps peace is public security. Or calm serenity. In the growing field of peace studies, the concepts of negative peace and positive peace are helpful concepts as we grapple with the definition of peace.

Negative peace is the absence of war or violence. It is frequently maintained by social and political repression of dissident individuals, groups, religions or cultural minorities. In this context "peace-keeping" is often accomplished by military power and coercive force.

Positive peace, on the other hand, refers to social and cultural situations in which exploitation is either minimized or eliminated entirely. Overt forms of violence are absent. Structural violence is also absent. Because the concept of positive peace is more difficult to articulate than negative peace, individuals and groups often question the possibility of peace without coercion or violence.

The emerging peace-studies discipline identifies peace-building as the development of non-exploitive social structures sustained over time. Other languages offer insight in defining the parameters of positive peace. The Greek word for peace, *eirene,* connotes a triple reality of peace, social harmony and justice. The Arabic *salaam* and the Hebrew *shalom* carry connotations of well-being, wholeness, abundance and harmony within one's self, as well as harmony in social relationships and the absence of violence. The Sanskrit word *shanty* refers to spiritual tranquillity and an integrated balance of inner and outer ways of being in the world. In Chinese, the word *ping* carries the nuances of harmony and the achievement of unity from within diversity. Finally, the Russian word *mir* means peace with the nuances of both the village community and the entire world.

While many dedicated individuals have created and continue to create significant and hopeful changes within their local communities, isolated individual actions are usually incapable of creating long-term, sustainable peaceful communities. Concerted primary prevention efforts are essential to destroy the breeding grounds of violence. To do this work of ending violence and creating positive peace, the entire community must be involved. The elimination of structural violence is one place to begin. Another is the successful treatment and healing of individuals already suffering from previous encounters with violence. Helping to deter individuals at risk from entering the cycle of violence is yet another.

Surely there are other important places to start. When a whole community begins to talk, with each person free to share his or her wisdom about successful peace-building, new interventions can be tried to stop or lessen violence while also creating a peace-filled environment. We remain hopeful that a more peaceful millennium is possible if we begin to create peace in our local communities. When we speak of peace-building from now on, we shall always be referring to positive peace.

We share the optimism of Thich Nhat Hanh. Peace begins with each one of us and moves out into the community. Peace is not only the desired end or goal. Peace is every step of the journey. By learning how to *be peace,* we participate in the creation of lasting, sustainable, abundant peace. Choosing in our own lives to opt for the spiritual journey of peace-building, we become resources to others who also seek to find ways out of the seemingly impenetrable maze of our human legacy of violence.

Peace-making in the domain of public health

Much may be learned about reducing violence and building peace from the discipline of public health. A central concern of public health is prevention. Institutionalized public health generally utilizes a team of clinicians, statisticians and researchers to prevent disease. Teams address complex public-health problems and issues where multiple causative factors must be identified and manipulated to change or eliminate the problems. The diversity of the disciplines involved in public health allows practitioners to look at systemic issues as well as individual ones. To prevent polio, for example, public-health approaches have included developing and issuing a vaccine, quarantines, cleaning up public-use water facilities such as swimming pools and physical therapy for individuals who were already afflicted with the wasted muscle structures caused by the illness.

Recently the attention of the public-health field has shifted to address injury, poverty and violence. Although violence is different from purely medical causes of disease, it still impacts the public health of the nation and its people. Due to the failure of other political and societal forces in addressing and successfully intervening to combat the growing wave of domestic violence inside the United States, public-health organizations have begun to organize programmes of research and intervention. Along with treatment and cures, the third goal of organizational public health – prevention – remains consistent. In human lives and in human systems it is usually more cost-effective to prevent a problem from developing than it is to treat it once it has become endemic within an individual or society. A prevention strategy can and must be developed for violence.

There are three kinds of prevention strategies. *Primary preventions* include those intended to prevent the onset of disease. Primary prevention is usually directed at the general population, with occasional targeting of high-risk populations. *Secondary prevention* relies on screening and early detection of conditions or a disease in a population. The goal of secondary prevention is to catch a condition early enough that an intervention can rapidly restore a person to a state of wellness. *Tertiary prevention* involves those who already have the condition in question, and it is intended to protect individuals from further injury. This form of prevention is meant to prevent the condition from causing long-term disability or death.

Many individual, environmental and cultural factors contribute to the use of violence. These multiple risk factors for violence – a number of different causes, none of which may be sufficient alone – suggest why some individuals living in poverty turn to violence but some do not, and why an abused child may or may not become an abuser in turn. Medicine and public health provide similar examples. Simply being exposed to the virus that causes the common cold does not necessarily mean that one will get sick. Other factors, such as the type of exposure, length of exposure, general nutrition and one's own immune system, all affect whether or not a specific individual will catch a cold. Protective factors also exist to help prevent violence.

The public health community has identified several resiliency factors that protect individuals in stressful situations. This field of inquiry is still growing, and new factors continue to be identified. Important in primary prevention programmes, resiliency factors may be individual traits such as good social and problem-solving skills, a sense of purpose, good self-esteem, intelligence, a sense of humour or curiosity. These traits may be learned or inherent. Resiliency factors may also be found in a family that has an effective conflict management style, a caring and supportive environment with positive interactions, adequate space and high expectations of children. A resilient community is one that has a low crime rate, that is supportive of its members and that promulgates consistent messages about the importance of non-violence. The resiliency of a community will impact its ability to reduce violence and build a culture of peace.

Peace-making and community development
One of the basic tenets of community development is empowerment of people to solve their own problems. It encourages involving people at a grassroots level. Community development workers have a toolkit of skills they use to do their work. One is to survey the community to identify the assets available – the parks, schools, employment opportunities, health-care agencies, food outlets, housing, public transportation access points, faith centres, after-school programmes, recreational facilities and other community assets, including persons, programmes or environmental features that serve as potential assets. Development workers can also assess the risk factors of a community by locating the centres for gang activity, areas of illicit drug sales and prostitution, alcohol outlets, gun dealers and places with frequent police calls. Overlapping these two surveys gives a good picture of the community and provides the information needed to assist in planning for prevention and development.

Information obtained from the surveys can be used to ascertain community strengths and encourage community members to continue building on these strengths, helping to promote a culture of peace.

> *Surveys worked in Vallejo, California*
> A group called the Fighting Back Partnership (www.fight-back.org) worked at reducing crime and violence in the city by addressing the role of alcohol in violence and promoting a community-based response to control alcohol outlets. In Vallejo, alcohol or other drugs were involved in 70 to 80 percent of violent acts.
>
> The partnership also helped neighbourhoods develop coalitions in order to revitalize their neighbourhoods, mobilizing the faith community and the police force in their efforts. Through these efforts they established a community economic development programme that converted former alcohol outlets into other businesses that promote the health and wellness of the community.
>
> When they learned that a new gas station being built in the community was applying for a liquor licence to sell alcohol on the premises, they successfully organized the neighbourhood to attend the city council meeting with their concerns. Because they had done a community survey, they knew that they did not need another alcohol outlet in the neighbourhood. They were successful. While the neighbourhood needed a new gas station, it did not need another alcohol outlet. They convinced the owner that they were serious about boycotting the station if he continued with his quest to secure a liquor licence. The city council listened to their concerns and denied the request. The owner chose not to appeal the decision made by the council.

Prevention spectrum

One tool we have found helpful in organizing community efforts is the Prevention Spectrum created by Larry Cohen and associates at the Prevention Institute in Oakland, California. The Spectrum was designed to develop more effective programmes to prevent injuries. It helps practitioners think comprehensively as they develop prevention initiatives. The Spectrum has six inter-related action levels that support each other and provide for a collaborative, sustainable approach to improved health and safety. The six levels incorporate prevention targeted to individuals as well as legislation to promote wellness. The key to the success of the Spectrum is its emphasis on comprehensive, community-wide collaboration across all disciplines.

Figure 1: Spectrum of Prevention

Level of Spectrum	Definition of Level	Example
1. Strengthen Individual Knowledge and Skills	Enhance an individual's capability of preventing violence and building peace	Conflict resolution training workshops for individuals
2. Promote Community Education	Reach groups of people with information and resources to promote peace-building	Mass media campaign
3. Educate Providers	Inform providers who will transmit skills and knowledge to others	Conflict resolution training workshops for teachers and other providers of service to the community
4. Foster Coalitions and Networks	Bring together groups and individuals for broader goals and greater impact	Family Violence Council made up of all agencies that work with victims of domestic abuse
5. Change Organizational Practices	Adopt regulations and shape norms to build peace	Industry-wide policy to allow family leave for parents to attend child's school functions
6. Influence Policy Legislation	Develop strategies for laws and policies that promote peace in local communities	Lobby for adequate state funding to assure access to quality education and health care for all children

Cohen developed the Spectrum of Prevention in 1983, refining it while directing a local health department in Contra Costa County, California, where it was used in injury prevention programmes for youth. Because the Spectrum emerged from practice, it is a practical and helpful tool. It is based on the belief that complex community problems require comprehensive solutions that involve all sectors of society.

Every chapter of this book uses the Spectrum, adapted to peace-building activities. One of the strengths of the Spectrum is that it promotes collaborative work across disciplines while carefully attending to multiple levels of approaches – from individual skill development to changing organizational policies and effecting changes in legislation.

Given this information on the basic principles and vocabulary necessary for creating a culture of peace, read on to see how these principles may be applied to build peace in your own community. We believe in developing a culture of peace through primary prevention measures, using a strengths-based approach to community development. We encourage interdisciplinary collaboration that involves as many different individuals and groups as feasible within any given community.

Each group or community that wishes to effect community-wide change and transformation must put into place a plan for community education and planned measurable change. Such a plan will likely involve change in organizational practices as well as laws, ordinances and regulations. The community must actively commit itself to doing whatever is needed to promote peace. Broad-based community action requires us to ask, "Who needs to be included for our work to be both effective and sustainable?" Such an approach is essential to effective planning and implementing peace-promoting actions and conditions. In addition, broadly constructed community coalitions usually ensure that resources are managed in such a way that they are not wasted in costly, multiple-agency duplication of services.

In the next chapters we will show how various sectors of our society can work at building peace in the community. The ones we highlight are education, health, faith communities, media, community-based organizations and the public sector. We believe that a community working together can create a culture of peace.

At the end of each chapter there are questions for reflection. These questions were written specifically for application in a local community. The best way to use this book is to work collaboratively.

Happy peace-making!

2. Education: Teaching a Culture of Peace

A ten-year-old boy sat in my office explaining to me why he kept falling asleep in school. I knew his home life was difficult, with multiple experiences of abuse and witnessing his mother being beaten by his step-father. Through tears he told about needing to stay awake at night to protect his mother. He explained, as best he could, that he loved her and that he would do anything to stay with her – including being beaten himself.

Each of us needs to feel loved and secure. We all need to experience a sense of belonging. As educators we hope that our students will find such love, security and belonging from both good relationships and supportive environments. Children cannot learn if they do not feel safe in their environments. Are we prepared to rise to the challenge of helping them fill this need for safety and acceptance in socially healthy and positive ways?

Introduction

Schools and educational institutions for all ages are uniquely positioned within our communities to make strategic differences that impact the well-being of tomorrow's societies. A culture of peace can be instrumental in moving us from being violence-centred and reactive in our educational approaches to becoming peace-loving and proactive in developing members for a civil society.

We often point our fingers at the schools and say, "Do something!" But schools do not operate in a vacuum. Though there are significant actions that schools can undertake to promote peace, without a supportive community their efforts will be in vain. Addressing the by-products of violence is not primarily a school problem; it is a community-wide problem. What happens in the community spills over into the school. What happens at school spills over into the community. While schools need to learn to work with each other, they also need to work across disciplines in order to effect change in the community that will impact the school as well. Schools are uniquely situated in the community to work collaboratively at peace-building efforts.

The strenghts-based, peace-building actions recommended for the education sector and highlighted in this chapter are listed below.

1. Developing peace-building behaviours among students while nurturing positive family involvement

Individual behaviour modification and personal change strategies involve teaching skills and providing information that help students stay safe in school and in their homes and neighbourhood. Our research suggests that many model programmes focus not only on preventing violence but also on building positive skills in students and adults to build a peace-centred future. Among these positive skills are:

- *Healthy verbal skills:* To help children develop verbal skills to manage difficult situations such as anger and frustration, schools can teach friendship skills, conflict resolution, anger management, empathy, impulse control and celebration of differences to all students from kindergarten through age 17-18. These teachings may take the form of separate curriculums. There are many published curricula from which to choose: samples appear in the bibliography. Skill acquisition may also be incorporated into the academic curriculum. Every subject area can include conflict management principles – from problem-solving skills in mathematics to language arts or history projects on Nobel Peace laureates. Investing time in teaching these skills will buy more time on task because less time will be spent on discipline and relationship problems.
- *Conflict management and mediation:* We need to learn how to get along with those with whom we disagree, those who make us angry and those who challenge our sense of safety. Conflict management and mediation skills for both adults and children build resiliency. Resilient individuals and children are less prone to violence.

While working as a social worker in a local middle school late one afternoon, I was asked by the assistant principal to talk with two students. He heard a rumour that they were preparing for a fight in the parking lot after school. I invited both young men to my office and they admitted that, indeed, they planned to fight each other after school.

We talked for a while, trying to discover what the fight was about. It became clear that neither boy wanted to fight. In fact, neither boy had done anything to the other that necessitated a fight. Through the middle school rumour mill, they heard that Timmy wanted to fight Tommy and when Tommy heard this challenge he had no recourse but to say, "Yeah, I can whip him." In this school, student crowds collect whenever a student fight is rumoured. Unless something unusual happened, today would be no exception. Student peer pressure would force Timmy and Tommy into fighting even though neither of them wanted to fight nor understood what the fight was about. Neither of them wanted to be viewed as the one who backed down. They were looking at me with eyes of desperation, silently pleading for a way to get out of this situation and save face at the same time.

Conflict mediation skills are vital for children. Using problem-solving skills and empathic listening, Timmy and Tommy were able to find a solution to their problem. It helped to have a neutral third party who could coach them through the process. They agreed not to fight. They agreed on a statement that both could use when their friends asked them if they planned to fight. Better still, in the course of the school year, they became friends.

This incidents, and others like it, underscore for me that kids really do not want to fight. But they don't want to look weak either. We need to teach them how to resolve conflicts in peaceful ways that keep their self-esteem and self-respect intact.

- *Personal civility:* Pre-school and day-care providers can teach basic civility – how to share, respect one another, be thoughtful and kind, and how to join a group appropriately. The earlier these skills are introduced, the better. In the United States, recent research on "bullies" indicates that these children are more isolated by their peer group and are more likely to move into juvenile crime and adult lives where significant amounts of time are spent in prison. Engaging elementary, middle school and secondary school teachers in the process of identifying bullying behaviour is essential. Even more essential is planning specific, measurable interventions that will assist the young bully to find pleasure in more acceptable peer activities.

As we adults think about teaching children specific skills in personal civility, basic respect for the rights of others, acceptance of and enjoyment of the challenges of diverse friendships, anger management and conflict resolution, it is essential to consider the specific developmental abilities and needs for each age group of students.

In 1980, Bridgework Theater (www.bridgework.org) was formed to create and perform plays that build bridges between people, fostering attitudes and ideas that help to solve a community's most urgent problems. In the past twenty years, Bridgework's critically acclaimed plays have been presented to 2 million children throughout the United States. Plans are to reach 250,000 children per year by developing additional teams of actors, training teachers and interacting with students via video, Internet and on-site actor/educators. *Tough*, a play for students in grades 1-4, and *Crossing the Line*, for grades 5-8, deal with ways of understanding bullying and standing up to bullying behaviours. Practical solutions comprise including and being friends with people who could be or are being bullied as well as joining others to disapprove of bullying and inappropriate teasing behaviours. A third option is to ask for help from adults.

> *Friends* (grades 1-4) teaches conflict resolution through managing anger, identifying emotions, and specifying actions to solve a problem. *Trading Places*, also for grades 1-4, helps students empathize and identify with peers who are from different backgrounds. This understanding can be a key component in resolving conflict. *Krista's Enemy*, for grades 5-8, models peer mediation and conflict resolution using an eight-step process.

- *Diversity appreciation and tolerance:* Children and adults are interacting more and more with people who are different from them.

  These differences may involve ethnicity, race, age, disability, sexual orientation, religious affiliation or economic status. Increasingly, individual and communal differences are found among neighbours and friends. The more we teach our children how to appreciate the unique realities of others, the better prepared they will be to live in culturally diverse settings.

> M. Agosin and E. Sepulveda document decades of correspondence between two women who were born in Chile, in South America and later needed to immigrate to the United States. One of them was a Roman Catholic girl being educated in a local convent. The second was a Jewish girl whose parents had fled Europe for safety. These young women met in 1965 and began a correspondence that would carry them beyond national boundaries and religious differences. Their letters contain the celebration of their growing friendship and their reliance upon each other as they enter northern colleges and universities. Today both women are tenured faculty members in North American academies and their friendship still sustains them in the face of prejudice against women whose first language was Spanish.

In attempting to live peacefully with others whose cultural heritage is different from our own, it is important to realize that another's cultural rules about good behaviour may be contradictory to those of our own culture. For example, in some cultures, it is important to maintain eye contact in order to communicate a willingness to listen to what the other person is saying. But in other cultures, it is important to avert the eyes as a sign of showing respect.

Learning the rules about physical comfort zones is also important. In some cultural groups, physical closeness signals friendship. In other groups, this same degree of physical closeness signals intrusiveness. For individuals inside each group to befriend others, they must recognize each other's signals, discuss and honour them. Significant gender issues also come into play. Appropriate male-female behaviour in one culture may be considered inappropriate or even abusive in another.

When people from two cultures begin to interact with each other, each may misunderstand the intentions of the other. Both may judge the other culture as rude and inhospitable to strangers. However, when both groups come to understand that a cultural variation is at play, they can begin to adjust their expectations and judgments of each other. Role-playing and cultural demonstrations in the classroom can assist children to learn how other people do it. In one of her classrooms, Ruth asked her students to demonstrate "proper physical distance from the professor". Then she asked them to demonstrate "proper physical distance from their best friend". This visual demonstration enabled students to understand that even in a college classroom, teacher and student may misunderstand each other because of cultural patterning that they have brought to the classroom. Children and adults come away with a new appreciation for the reality that there are many "right" ways to behave and interact with others that demonstrate respect and appreciation.

Economic status also creates diversity within a culture. What may be acceptable behaviour for members inside the elite class may be totally unacceptable behaviours for members of the working poor. Teaching children and adults of diverse economic strata about how to interact with each other is vitally important in situations where we wish to assist communities to begin to make changes in society. It is important to teach children and adults about how to interact respectfully with marginalized individuals. It is also important to understand one's own vulnerabilities and weaknesses, in order to appreciate the strengths of others.

> As a school social worker, I often see the pain and impact of insensitivity. "Mrs H, you don't wanna go in there. If you ever have to take a student home in that neighbourhood drop them off on the corner and let them walk home." "Why?" I asked. "Because, they don't like white people. Actually, they don't like nobody, and if you're white they really don't like you." "Is it like that in your neighbourhood?" "It used to be that way. You can go there now. But when I was younger even the police did not want to go in there."
> This conversation took place while I was driving a 13-year old boy home from school one afternoon. He was having trouble with class work and getting along with his peers. Indeed, one week later he was expelled for fighting and was subsequently transferred to an alternative middle school for children who are unable to manage in a traditional school setting.
> What I learned from this young boy, who grew up in subsidized city housing for the poor, was that it is not easy for a young child to modify successful and adaptive behaviours in order to succeed in school, where appropriate behaviours are different from those needed for survival on the streets. To ask young children to become social and emotional chameleons in order to survive in two such different environments is to set them up for failure.

- *Courageous acts of kindness:* Bullying programmes address the role of bystanders and offer training on how to resist a bully non-violently. Bystanders are people who witness a violent act. In the school setting, bystanders are those who witness a bully on the playground or watch the extortion of lunch money. Studies of acts of perpetration show that the behaviour of the bystanders often determines how far the bully will go in carrying out an act of violence. Bullies love an audience. All it takes is for one bystander to take a positive action, however, and others will follow. Children need to be taught how to intervene appropriately in a bullying situation and be supported in their endeavours. Reinforcement by teachers and school administrators through positive helping and courageous acts of kindness can be extremely important in calming and changing the tone of a volatile situation, thus promoting a culture of peace.

Children who move from bystanders to helpers tend to develop a strong moral character with a fundamental sense of empathy for others. This suggests that helping behaviours can be modelled, learned, taught and reinforced. One would hope these behaviours would be taught within the family setting. Not many children, however, are getting this type of training in the home. Schools and religious communities are positioned to underscore the importance of doing the right thing at the right time through role modelling and creative lessons.

Another significant area of activity is strengthening the home environment. The ideal scenario is for homes across the globe to offer nurturing environments. Sadly, in the United States, for instance, the surgeon general's report on youth violence states that children are safer at school than anywhere else. Despite highly publicized incidents of school shootings across the United States, children are less likely to be killed at school than at home or in their neighbourhood. Other less violent cultures than the United States place a high priority on extended family involvement. Care-giving becomes an act where many loved ones (and even neighbours) value safety for their children both at home and school.

- *Positive adult role modelling:* The importance of positive adult modeling cannot be over-emphasized. Young children pattern their behaviour after the adults they admire, love and respect. Experiments with nursery school students have demonstrated conclusively that when adults acted aggressively towards a life-sized doll and were not punished or reprimanded, the children consequently behaved in more aggressive ways towards the doll as well.

Children not only hear what we say as we interact with them, they also observe a much more complex reality: how we live our lives in proximity to them is a more powerful teacher than what we say.

- *Positive peer relationship monitoring:* Care-giving adults need to set boundaries that let children and teens know that teachers and parents care about whom they "hang out with". The most critical risk factor for violence is the behaviour of our children's peers. The more time kids have to "hang around" and do nothing, the more likely they are to get into trouble, use drugs or become involved in sexual activity.

In the United States, for example, the hours of three to six in the afternoon are the most dangerous hours for young people. Generally, schools finish mid-afternoon while many parents do not return from work until late in the evening. As the children get older, they are often left unsupervised or under-supervised during this time.

It is important for all significant adults in a child's life to pay attention to his or her activities and friendships. It is especially important for parents to know their children's friends. All adults should encourage healthy peer relationships among children and adolescents. Children and adolescents need reasonable and clear expectations for their behaviour. They need respectful and consistent discipline. Especially, they need to learn their culture's system of acceptable and unacceptable behaviours.

- *Healthy media and technology consumers:* Both adults and children benefit from becoming critical consumers of the media. Parents especially need to monitor the amount and kinds of violence their children are exposed to on TV, videos, internet, computer games and interactive video games. Every parent should be aware of the impact of TV and other violent media on children. In North American television, violent role models influence young, impressionable minds.

We need to teach our children to "talk back" to the television. While parenting has been a humbling experience for me, I celebrated a small success the day I walked into the room in time to hear my ten-year-old daughter emphatically respond to the commercial she was watching on the TV: "Just who are you trying to kid?" Children who are taught critical thinking skills are more able to cope with the bombardment of messages from the variety of media that assail them daily.

It is essential for parents to be involved in the lives of their children and to take responsibility for the education of their children by partnering with the school. Parent-teacher organizations can think beyond fund-raising to promote opportunities for parent conversations among themselves and with teachers. They can organize a "parent corner" at school where parents can find resources about parenting amid the rapid changes happening in their lives.

2. Fostering community education

Providing information to the general public is an important component of building peace. Schools and academic institutions of higher education are uniquely situated to provide that public education. The education sector can promote:

- *Mass media campaigns:* Community education can be done through mass media campaigns. In an after-school teen programme in California, teens were taught how to prepare public service announcements utilizing the latest technological equipment. They wrote a script focusing on how to reduce violence in their community and filmed it. Local television stations agreed to air it without charging a fee.
- *Town hall meetings:* Community education can also be done through town hall meetings hosted by a school or

university. Schools can utilize their building space for such meetings, facilitating community conversations by sharing both space and personnel.
- *Special educational events:* Schools can offer "awareness evenings" to interested community members. If school personnel are aware of gang activity in the community because it gets played out in their hallways and playgrounds, they can host a special event to bring this information to the attention of both families and community leaders. They can also develop close working relationships with local law enforcement officials, inviting them to the event and consulting with them before and after. Law enforcement officers benefit from these contacts, as do school administrators, teachers and students.

3. Continuing education with professional colleagues

It takes the teamwork of all those working with young people to establish a positive environment where the messages we give them are consistent. Teaching young people how to resolve conflicts peacefully will not happen overnight and it will not happen without the help of professional colleagues. Everyone who comes in contact with students needs to be trained in peaceful resolution of conflicts. School employees, as well as other adults in the community providing services to students, can receive training in conflict de-escalation and transformation as well as other peace-building skills.

> From the Guatemala Mennonite Church comes an example of teachers who realized they themselves needed to learn to deal with conflict more effectively before they could train the children to do so.
> In a school culture of authoritarianism and violence, discipline relies on shouting and expulsion. The Guatemalan Mennonite Church decided to offer a workshop to train teachers how to teach transformation skills to children in conflict. The teachers admitted that they had their own problems, and so they first

> undertook training themselves. Now they work every Thursday afternoon with fourth, fifth and sixth graders on a conciliation curriculum to train student peace-makers.
>
> Discipline problems are now referred to a teacher who talks to the student about alternative conduct. Teachers also facilitate meetings with parents about contentious issues such as child abuse.

4. Facilitating communication and networking across sectors

It is important to bring together a coalition of community agencies to improve the chances of reaching goals and expanding the impact of the peace-making effort. Coalitions can be more efficient in the use of community resources and lessen the possibility of duplicating services. When agencies work together, they create a unique synergy in meeting community needs and promoting a culture of peace. Coordinating institutional programmes encourages the sharing of strategies and resources.

- *Facilitate collective social action:* If we are serious about wanting to do something about the violence that surrounds us, we must take logical steps to facilitate social change and peace-building. By inviting physicians, mental health workers, social service professionals, police, educators, clergy and other interested individuals to work collaboratively, we can increase the impact of our social action and community change efforts.
- *Establish safety networks:* It is important for schools to foster community coalitions and networks in the community by bringing together the people necessary to ensure students' physical safety. Many schools cooperate with local police departments who provide school resource officers who work in the school.

Salinas, California, city officials found that there was a 50 percent dropout rate for students between grades nine and twelve, many of them young women. To counter this high dropout rate, the city established a federally funded "Weed and Seed" programme that organizes an annual retreat for all sixth-grade girls. Each girl invites her mother or another significant female adult. During the retreat, the pairs undertake activities together to increase their communication skills. The programme that started as a one-day conference, now has its own curriculum and meets twice a month, providing information that will assist girls in their transition to womanhood. The programme helps with the transition from elementary school to middle school and provides information on community resources available for educational, recreational and leisure activities. Perhaps most importantly, the programme encourages girls to stay in school and to consider getting a college education.

Some communities have developed after-school programmes that use the facilities of local churches. Fellowship halls are transformed into basketball courts and volunteers provide academic tutoring for neighbourhood children after school.

- *Partner across educational systems:* Local elementary, middle and high schools can be encouraged to work with post-secondary education professionals. Often there are people on college or university campuses with expertise on various issues relevant to creating a culture of peace in the education system. For example, Goshen College students are actively encouraged to include volunteer work in the community as part of their educational programme. Students often mentor a child from the local school. These relationships may include academic tutoring and learning English, as well as demonstrating appropriate social behaviour at stores, restaurants or recreational events. The goal in these relationships is to form a friendship in which the college student can make a permanent and positive change in the life experience of the child.

Higher educational institutions have the capacity to do research on community needs and how to meet them. They can also conduct evaluation projects to ascertain what is working. Their students can do the leg-work required for data collection under the supervision of experts. In addition,

university students and professors make good tutors for school children. Many are looking for ways to do community service such as reading to children.
- *Encourage business involvement:* In some communities, businesses adopt a local school and provide mentors. Mentoring programmes have been proven to be effective in deterring violent behaviour in children. Many students come from single-parent families or families with heavy substance abuse. These students benefit from having an adult encourage them to reach their full potential. Single parents appreciate having another adult interact with their child.

Businesses can also provide personnel to help strengthen business-school ties. What would happen if a business allowed employees an extended lunch break one day a week with an at-risk child? The employees could go to a school, read to a child, have lunch, tutor or just "hang out" with them.

> The CARES programme in northern Indiana offers an outstanding model of what happens for at-risk children when community organizations work together (www.elkhart.k12.in.us). School personnel match adult volunteers with children in the school. The adult agrees to spend one half hour a week with the child at school. They may tutor the child in an academic subject or they may spend the time playing a game or talking. Some local businesses give their employees permission to take an extra half-hour on their lunch break every week in order to provide this service for the school. A local hospital adopted the elementary school down the street. Many churches have each adopted local schools. One church has over seventy volunteers a week in a school. Schools report that children with sporadic attendance manage to make it to school on the day their tutor is coming. In addition to benefiting the children, the volunteers are quick to admit that they receive far more from this community service than they give.

- *Nurture public sector partnerships:* Thinking collaboratively about alternatives to suspension benefits everyone – the student, family, school and community. Community-based interventions for youths struggling socially and educationally can make a long-term difference in their self-esteem and behaviours.

> The Second Chance Youth Programme in Salinas, California, aims at reducing gang involvement and gang violence. Jazz-up is a programme for 14-to 18-year-old youth that provides an opportunity to do community service. Students are referred to Jazz-up by probation officers, with community service hours being one of the terms of probation. Teens are also referred by the school system. When students are expelled from school, they cannot return until they do a certain number of hours of community service and receive counselling. Most of the community service is spent in beautification projects, particularly in low-income neighbourhoods.
>
> DEFY (Drug Education For Youth) is another programme of Second Chance. In collaboration with the city and the youth attorney's office, 32 9-to-12-year-olds are selected from the at-risk areas of the city. In addition, teen mentors (ages 14 to 18) from the same area of town are selected to work with the younger children. Together they go to a week-long camp for an introduction to leadership development, goal setting, decision-making and other skills. Phase 2 of the programme allows them to meet once a month to reinforce what they learned at camp, to take them places that will broaden their horizons and to continue to build relationships.

5. Ensuring positive learning practices
- *Nurture and ensure environmental safety:* One of the most significant policy issues in schools today is the need for students to learn in a safe environment. The task of the

school is to provide a safe environment for the students so they are able to learn. To ensure this safety, schools and universities continually assess their existing practices and policies to address both emergency and daily safety issues. These policies should reflect the values of strengths-based peace-building.
- *Offer wellness services:* By partnering with local health care providers and the public health department, schools can host on-site health clinics, including provision of immunizations. This partnership is one step towards keeping kids healthy and attending school.
- *Develop restorative disciplinary strategies:* Developing strategies for restorative discipline and alternatives to suspension and expulsion are important for schools to meet the needs of all students. By restorative discipline we mean helping the student understand the effects of the offending behaviour on the school community as well as on themselves, while working towards reintegrating him or her into the classroom as a productive and contributing member. Engaging local colleges and universities to be involved in this endeavour will strengthen the strategies. State legislatures can be encouraged – or even pressured – to fund creative thinking about restorative discipline.
- *Require peace-building in-service training for school staff:* Sometimes well-meaning adults aggravate tense situations. All adults who come into contact with students – from school bus drivers to cafeteria workers, teachers to para-professionals, secretaries to administrators – can be taught skills in conflict resolution, anger management, empathy and tolerating differences. They also need to be able to recognize children who are in trouble and have the necessary knowledge of community resources to help them.
- *Ensure that organizational policies and practices are prevention-oriented:* Many schools employ metal detectors, surveillance cameras, and uniformed officers to prevent violence. It is good for a school to have a crisis plan and to improve security and limit access to school buildings.

School security experts admit, however, that if a student wants to take a gun to school, metal detectors and uniformed officers will not deter him or her. Crisis plans and metal detectors are reactive measures and they have a limited role. We might ask ourselves – and our children – why students do not feel safe.

> One preventive measure a school can easily implement is to determine where in the school violent behaviours are most likely to occur. Utilizing a building map, plot all the incidents of fighting, harassment, bullying and other behaviours that are serious enough to be referred to the administrator. With the information gleaned from this exercise, place adults in those "hot spots" in the building at those times of the day when the violence is most likely to occur. For example, if there are a large number of incidents on the playground or at the bus drop-off area when the students arrive, strategically place adults in that area at that time. An adult presence helps deter acts of violence and creates an environment in which students feel safe. Utilizing parent volunteers in this activity is a cost effective way of incorporating the community in proactive violence prevention efforts at the school.

6. Proposing healthy legislative change

Educators are advised to lobby state legislatures as well as departments of education to examine state educational policies to ascertain if they ensure a quality education for all. In influencing dialogue and legislative process, educators may:
- *Establish priority for societal peace-building efforts:* If we as a global society have the collective will, we can mobilize to significantly reduce violence and build a culture of peace. Are we ready to take on the challenge and make it a priority to expend our energy and resources on peace-building efforts? World resources have been harnessed to eradicate small pox, tuberculosis and polio. Yet

in the United States, for example, violence is currently the number one public health problem. Millions of dollars are invested to beautify our streets. It is time for civil societies to spend fiscal capital on peace-building efforts that make the streets safe and craft a culture of peace and justice for all.
- *Implement equitable funding models:* State funding formulas for education need to be scrutinized to ensure that all children have equal access to quality education. Funding patterns reflect societal values; our work is to make peace-building initiatives become values in our communities. Funding can provide increased resources for guidance counsellors and social workers to assist at-risk students.

Reflective questions
- What can you do to promote peace-building behaviours among students in your local school?
- What are some ideas you can use to nurture positive family involvement in school peace-building?
- How can you help build a positive learning environment?
- What are some tools you could use to facilitate communication and networking across different sectors of your community?
- What are some community peace-building education initiatives you could implement? Whose help do you need to enlist?
- What can be done to build better business-community involvement in peace education in your local school?
- What legislative policies and law changes could offer new opportunities for peace-building?
- What peace-building efforts are already being done in your school and community? Do more!

3. The Health Sector: A Front-Line for Building Peace

Little Amanda twisted in pain from the burns she suffered when mother's partner scalded her. I looked into her gray-brown eyes and wondered at the absence of an emotional response to her body's wounds. I wondered how an innocent seven-year-old child could be made to suffer so much. I knew her mother Anna well, as she had been in the hospital emergency room numerous times during the past month.

As a social worker, I was frequently asked to intervene in family violence cases. Anna was in an abusive relationship. Even though she received numerous bruises and lacerations, she refused to leave the abusive partner, saying, "He only hurts me when he drinks." It is difficult for a woman without family support and financial resources to leave an abusive relationship.

Introduction

In the 2001 world report on violence and health, the World Health Organization (WHO) discusses the forms and contexts of violence. The Report indicates that in the year 2000, 520,000 people were killed in acts of interpersonal (non-war) violence. The authors correctly note that official homicide rates do not tell the whole story since many "accidental deaths" are actually murders. For each person murdered in interpersonal acts of violence, many more individuals are physically injured or psychologically traumatized. Included in the category of interpersonal violence is abuse of children and the elderly as well as violence between intimate partners. When interpersonal violence is broken down into sub-groups, the magnitude of this issue becomes apparent. Below is a listing of some of the sub-groups:
- Young people between the ages of 10 and 29. The interpersonal violence includes a range of actions including bullying behaviours, physical fighting, serious forms of assault and homicide
- Violence against intimate partners includes acts of physical aggression such as beating, hitting or kicking: it

includes forced intercourse and psychological abuse such as intimidation, humiliation and controlling behaviours.
- Child abuse and neglect includes physical, sexual and psychological abuse as well as neglect.
- Abuse of the elderly includes physical, sexual, and psychological abuse. It also includes neglect and economic abuse.
- Sexual violence includes forced intercourse in marriage and dating relationships, rape by strangers, rape by family members or close family friends, systemic, organized rape during armed conflicts, sexual harassment, sexual abuse of children, forced prostitution and sexual trafficking, child marriage and violent acts against the sexual integrity of women, for example genital mutilation and obligatory inspections for virginity. It also includes rape in prisons, police custody situations and refugee camps.
- Self-directed violence includes suicide as well as physical mutilation of the body.

In addition to interpersonal violence, collective violence exists in multiple forms including wars, terrorism, forced displacement of people from their homes, gang warfare and gang rape as a weapon of war. The 20th century was one of the most violent periods in human history. According to the WHO, an estimated 191 million people lost their lives directly or indirectly as a result of conflict. More than half of these individuals were civilians. In addition, many millions more have been injured.

The WHO report suggests a variety of approaches to alleviate this problem. Those listed below may supplement the strengths-based agenda we suggest.

- Individual efforts to change the attitudes and behaviours of individuals who are already violent or who are at risk for becoming violent:
- Therapeutic programmes including counselling for victims of violence
- Therapeutic programmes for individuals at risk for hurting themselves

- Therapeutic programmes for offenders and perpetrators of violence
* Relationship approaches to deal with specific problems within families:
- parent training programmes, especially in situations where children are at risk for exposure to various forms of violence
- mentoring programmes, especially for children at risk for developing anti-social forms of behaviour
- family therapy programmes
- home visitation programmes with regular visits from a public health nurse or other health professional to support and provide guidance in parenting for families at risk
- training programmes in human relationship skills, including conflict-management skills
* Community-based efforts include raising public awareness of issues related to violence prevention as well as addressing social and material causes of violence in the local environment. Also included are care and support of victims:
- public education campaigns targeting entire communities
- modifications of the physical environment of neighbourhoods such as better lighting at night or creating safe playgrounds for children
- extra-curricular activities for young people, especially those at risk for violent behaviour
- training programmes for health care professionals to identify and respond appropriately to various forms of violence
- training programmes for personnel in hospitals, health care clinics and long-term care institutions for the elderly as well as health care practitioner offices
* Societal approaches include reducing structural violence in cultural, social and economic areas:
- policy changes to reduce social inequities and provide support for families
- efforts to change a culture of racism, sexism, gender, ethnic and religious discrimination

- legislative and judicial changes
- disarmament programmes
- international treaties

In reviewing this comprehensive but incomplete listing of violence issues which face individuals, communities and entire societies, it becomes clear that health-care providers can play a central role in assessing violence, treating victims or perpetrators of violence and in establishing individual or community based plans for peace-building activities. They can also select societal approaches to emphasize in their professional organizations.

While health-care personnel are often preoccupied with individual care, most physicians, nurses, clinical therapists and other health-related personnel understand their role in diagnosing and treating the aftermath of violence. Physicians and nurses, for example, are educated about recognizing the symptoms of intimate personal violence. Emergency room personnel are skilled at responding to the immediate trauma of weaponry-based violence. What is more difficult, however, is to persuade health-care practitioners in all settings that a necessary focus of their activities is the prevention of violence.

Increasing peace-building activities among overloaded medical personnel, including medical social workers and chaplains, can be a tough sell. Yet, who deals more directly with the impact of a violence-tolerant society than those in medical settings? Every day, medical personnel face the traumatic by-products of violence. The cost of living with violence takes a major psycho-social and financial toll on the social as well as the physical well-being of people across the globe.

One can question how the medical system, which remains in crisis in both the developed and developing countries, can advocate one more health-related issue. Yet, with many more Amanda situations facing the system each day, how can its members remain uninvolved in the public health benefits generated by building a societal culture of peace?

The strengths-based, peace-building actions recommended for the health sector and highlighted in this chapter include the following.

1. Create a restorative response to crisis

From emergency rooms to operating theatres, from pediatric clinics to gynecology offices, from school nurses to outpatient therapists, from massage therapists to alternative health-care consultants, health-care providers deal regularly with the aftermath of violence in the lives of their patients and their patients' families. In this context, medical personnel can think about restorative and long-term healing. Practitioners working at this level can:

- *Ensure a recovery safe haven for victims:* At medical centres the primary emphasis is often on responding to the physical needs of the victim. The psychological and social needs of the victim may be less helpfully addressed. When victims of violence experience a health-care practitioner's inability to be helpful, they experience what is now described as "sanctuary trauma". S.M. Silver has urged clinicians to create safe environments for those individuals who have had a traumatic experience of violence.

Recent trauma literature in the United States indicates that re-establishing safety is the number one priority for clinicians dealing with individuals who have experienced violence either recently or in the distant past. Creation of safe treatment environments is essential to the long-term healing of victims of violence. Safe environments include the following:

- Physical and environmental safety: Hospitals, for example, can pro-actively consider the safety needs of both personnel and patients in highly volatile areas such as emergency rooms that treat victims of violence.
- Psychological and emotional safety: Health-care personnel can empower victims of violence to reclaim as much personal power as possible within as rapid a time as possible. Patients and families can be actively consulted and taught about the options for care.
- Therapeutic safety: Health-care clinicians must adhere to their professional oaths and codes of conduct. Oversight groups in the various professions must be active and dili-

gent in removing professional credentials for health care practitioners who actively victimize their clients – by sexual misconduct, for example.

> An emergency room in a community hospital created a treatment room that was used exclusively for the treatment of victims of violence. It was designed to promote healing with soothing colours and soft lighting. Blanket warmers were available for victims with acute shock. Soothing scents and appropriate posters offered physical, emotional and spiritual healing for the whole person.

- *Examine personal and professional value orientation:* Health professionals are encouraged to confront and reflectively examine personal prejudices about specific groups or types of individuals they encounter. Prisoners, those recently released from prison, drug users and those who harm themselves are often among the least understood and most negatively judged and frequently rejected by health workers. This rejection is evident by slower treatment or being made to wait for help. It is evident in health-care personnel who make negative comments about these individuals. It can be seen in agency policies that actively deny access to health care to certain individuals. Health-care providers need to receive training and ongoing supervision in which they confront their own personal attitudes regarding victims and the victimization cycle. Health-care administrators and supervisors can assist all staff members to consider the way their own attitudes and behaviours negatively or positively affect the clinical resiliency outcomes for their clients. Blaming the victim can impair a health care professional's ability to provide objective and restorative care and judgmental attitudes produce a loss of confidence on the part of the victim. Pious and superior attitudes can exacerbate a patient's feelings of anger, loss and victimization. On the other hand, genuine care and

empathetic understanding can make a significant difference in promoting healing.
- *Foster resiliency of victims:* According to J. Herman therapists who work with survivors of violence are "called upon to bear witness to a crime". When working with victims of violence it is imperative that those in the helping profession help the victim understand and cope with the specific event or events of violence they experienced. It is important to help the victim understand the experience in a way that restores a sense of personal control.

Medical personnel can help victims by offering them a list of community resources appropriate to their circumstances, including financial assistances, as well as referrals to therapists experienced in working with victims. This assistance is essential in helping victims to break the cycle of violence.

> Restorative justice seeks healing of the victim and the community while holding an offender accountable for their actions, determining together how to make amends and ultimately returning the offender to the community as a productive citizen. An example of restorative justice in the USA is the Victim Offender Reconciliation Programme (VORP). This programme is designed to "make things as right as possible". VORP brings together both the victim and the offender with a neutral third party. The offender listens to how the victim experienced the offence and together they agree on restitution the offender can provide. The opportunity to talk with one's offender can bring about healing, when provided in a safe and caring environment.

2. Promote community education

In the United States, hospitals and health-care institutions have been forced in the past two decades to cut back on community education services because of political debates about how the community should spend its health-care dollars. In developing countries, especially those in war zones, health-care facilities are often non-existent. Long-term consequences occur, however, when we ignore primary prevention and peace-building education as integral components of a health-care environment or system.

Within the fields of pediatrics and family medicine, primary prevention of child abuse begins with a child's birth. Hospital nurses and volunteers teach problem-solving skills to new mothers and listen to parents express their concerns. New parents are encouraged to take time away from child care, leaving children with responsible care-givers so that they do not get frustrated to the point of harming their infants. In some communities, parents are encouraged to call parent support groups when they need relief from the pressures of parenting. These types of community programmes can help if parents feel that they are going to harm their children. Informal parenting support in many societies is done through strong ties with extended family.

> Since 1997 the state of Oklahoma, through the department of public health, has operated the Children First Programme. Its mission is to "produce healthy family members and enhance a family's ability to care for itself". Public-health nurses work with first time, low-income mothers beginning during pregnancy through the first two years of the child's life. In addition to providing primary-health-care assistance, the nurses also do activities that are designed to fit the developmental needs of first-time mothers and their extended families. Visits begin weekly and progress to bi-weekly and monthly during the first two years of the child's life. The programme assures proper health care and immunizations as well as providing parenting education and support for the family. In addition, the mothers learn about proper nutrition, health and safety information, and are linked to services for health care, child-care, mental health and job training as needed.

> An evaluation of the programme found that babies born to mothers in the programme were twice as likely to thrive in the first year of life as compared to babies of mothers not in the Children First programme. The immunization rate of babies in the programme exceeded the target immunization rates of the US surgeon general in the Healthy People 2010 Report.

- *Train for holistic life-style change:* Medical educators deal with the personal and environmental nature of wellness, targeting not only the individual, but his or her family as well. Community education can focus on healthy lifestyles, including good nutrition and adequate exercise.

Health-care providers can address primary prevention of violence through parenting programmes that inform them about different developmental stages and offer suggestions for how best to manage a child at each stage. These programmes last for eight to ten sessions. Some programmes also provide mentors for new or struggling parents. Educators can also encourage parents to develop their children's adaptive social skills by reading to their children and teaching them problem-solving skills to help them avoid violent behaviour.

3. Collaborate inter-professionally

Especially in urban areas members of the health-care professions (doctors, nurses, emergency medical technicians and psychotherapists) deal with the personal impacts of living in a violent society. Their effectiveness is enhanced when they work at creating interdisciplinary and collaborative relationships. Strong community-wide wellness models encourage communication, networking and collaboration across disciplines. Good public-health programmes focus on mobilizing a broad based support for promoting peace and wellness.

- *Increase cross-training effectiveness:* Community leaders are better prepared to collaborate if they:
- Learn the demographics of violence in the local community, recognizing the unspoken signs of violation in their

clients and asking clients about their experiences with violence. Trauma centres, law enforcement and crisis hotlines can work together to provide accurate statistics on violence in the community.
– Recognize the development of secondary trauma in people who work with victims of violence and foster the ability to ask others for help in returning to inner balance, harmony and compassion for the self as well as others. Providing opportunities for debriefing in a safe environment can help those who work closely with victims of violence maintain a sense of personal and professional well-being.
– Ask clients about the sources of violence in their lives and worked with them and community resource people (therapists, social workers, school personnel) to determine ways for growth in non-violent approaches to individual, family and community life.

4. Promote wellness activities that involve the community in peace-building

People who live in agrarian societies have long acknowledged the value of community. More recently, the United States Centre for Disease Control and Prevention has made a public effort to stress the health benefit of community involvement in violence prevention. To create a culture of peace, health sector personnel can:

- *Foster health/peace-building connections:* Health-care providers can enhance wellness through engaging diverse community members to participate in peace-building activities. Business leaders, civic groups, governmental agencies, educators and religious leaders can be involved in finding long-term solutions to the epidemic of violence.

Rachel Naomi Remen demonstrates the wisdom of preparing young physicians to work in today's complex health-care system, encouraging them to develop networks for political action that build and enhance needed services for survivors of violence. For political action to have a signifi-

cant impact, local community leaders must work together on community awareness of – and commitment to – their peace-building efforts.
- *Know referral resources:* Health-care providers should be aware of the resources available in the community to heal the wounds of violence and build a culture of peace. These resources include preventive, therapeutic and educational services for those who have been victimized. Service providers may include psychiatric social workers, chaplains and pastors as well as social service agencies. Brochures and agency literature in waiting rooms provide information about preventive and healing services available in the community. Service providers can work together to prepare updated information about resources and services.

5. Encourage organizational sensitivity to positive wellness policies and practices

Organizations can address policies and procedures that increase the wellness of the community, promoting family-friendly practices like family leave, sick leave and access to quality child care. The health sector can undertake the following:
- *Develop clear crisis procedures:* Health-care professionals and institutions can develop clear and well-informed procedures for managing violent clients as well as for treating victims of violence. The policies and procedures for identifying at-risk individuals need to be clear and readily available for all personnel. Well-developed referral networks for social services, counselling and legal services are also important. Health-care providers in diverse settings need to be able to assess the role that violence plays in a victim's life and how, when and where to intervene.
- *Encourage health-conscious policies in employment:* Both employees and employers benefit from clear health-promotion programmes. Most people spend more time at their place of employment than anywhere else. Pro-

grammes designed to assure healthy life-styles of employees yield many benefits, including increased productivity. Providing day-care facilities for working parents can promote the well-being of employee families. To promote staff wellness, medical centres can offer healthy food and drink options in their staff rooms and cafeterias. They can also provide exercise rooms and use of physical therapy resources such as whirlpools and massages to help employees eliminate the strain of their profession. Creating flexible schedules and offering job-sharing options can also reduce the impact of work-induced stress.

6. Lobby for improved social policies that ensure wellness for all

Health-care personnel can work at making legislative changes that promote a culture of peace. To influence the legislative process they can:

- *Mobilize professional associations:* Professional associations have traditionally been highly effective at effecting change. A network such as the American Medical Association enjoys significant political clout that can be used for lobbying. Doctors, nurses and social workers can advocate on behalf of survivors of violence. They and their professional associations are in a position to testify to the need for change and, as they can, work for public policies that promote equal and equitable access to health care for all.

Reflective questions
- What strategies can be used to increase medical team awareness of the social factors that impact their patients?
- How can medical personnel increase their knowledge of the health/peace correlation?
- What organizational practices need to change to improve family wellness?
- What are some activities the health-care sector could provide to promote a culture of peace?

- Can you suggest improved social policies and practices that will ensure that wellness is available to all?
- What personal and communal resources do health-care workers and therapists need in order to stay committed to helping clients deal with the aftermath of violence in their individual, family and community lives?
- What spiritual resources can be developed by clinicians to avoid burnout or secondary post-traumatic stress disorder?

4. The Religious Sector: Moral Compass for Peace-Building

> Forgiveness is an act of much hope, and not despair. It is to hope in the essential goodness of people and to have faith in their potential to change. It is to bet on that possibility. Forgiveness is not opposed to justice, especially if it is not punitive justice, but restorative justice, justice that does not seek primarily to punish the perpetrator, to hit out, but looks to heal a breach, to restore a social equilibrium that the atrocity or misdeed has disturbed.
> *Archbishop Desmond Tutu (Simpkinson, 2001)*

Introduction

While local, regional, national and international governments and their representatives have a responsibility to foster peaceful communities, faith institutions have a spiritual mandate to promote basic civility as well as unity, forgiveness, and the reconciliation of enemies. Expressing the ideal of "love for God, neighbour and self", religious communities can provide centres of spiritual nurture in which individuals and groups are called to transcend the acts and effects of violence.

In today's pluralistic world, it is impossible to conceive of peace-building initiatives that do not include religious representation and participation. Historically, members of the world's religious communities have used their spiritual identity and political power in the world for a wide variety of purposes. In some situations, religious groups and individuals have behaved in ways that created long-lasting legacies of religiously motivated violence. The 11th-century crusades, the expulsion of Sephardic Jews from Spain, the 16th-century burning of witches and heretics are all examples of religiously motivated violence. Religious motivation creates a particularly virulent form of violence in the world. Holy wars, fought in God's name for God's honour, are some of the bloodiest human wars in recorded history as religion has been misused in order to motivate and legitimate violence.

In other situations, however, religious individuals and communities have been powerful proponents of justice-based relationships within the religious and political order. Examples include Oscar Romero, the archbishop of El Salvador, in his final plea "to stop the killing" to the state and guerrilla armies of his nation; the church of La Merced in Nicaragua where religious faith supported social and economic reform to improve the lives of the poor; and the French-speaking monks of Tiburine who lived peacefully and contentedly among their Islamic neighbours during Algeria's civil war – treating the ill, weak, and wounded of any religion (or none at all) who came to their medical clinic. Perhaps the best-known example is that of the Hindu, Mahatma Gandhi, who inspired members of many religious faith communities, including Martin Luther King Jr and Ceasar Chavez, to use non-violent confrontation in the face of structural violence. Anglican Archbishop Desmond Tutu's work with the South African Truth and Reconciliation Commission is yet another example.

Religious individuals and religious groups who believe in peaceful relationships as a basic human need, believe also that peace-building action in the world is a spiritual, relational and theological mandate. These faith-motivated individuals and communities can take a central leadership role around the world in creating and sustaining the works of peace.

Among the strengths-based peace-building actions recommended for religious leaders and faith groups highlighted in this chapter are the following.

1. Foster a spirituality of reconciliation with self and others

If religious groups hope to make an impact in their peace-building approaches, they need to help individuals and their families learn ways of living peacefully with one another. To effect change at this level religious leaders can:

- *Nurture spirituality:* Religious groups often reflect the surrounding culture. As a result they may have limited possibilities for participating in radical peace-building actions in the world. The threat of disrupting organized religion is too great. However, spiritually intuitive individuals within any faith group often provide leadership and an urgent calling to ministries of peace-building. Spiritual leaders (whether institutionalized in organized religion or operating within a specific sense of call) are called to nurture values for peace-building among those who move within their spheres of influence. Dedicated members of a religious tradition can bring their personal conflict resolution and listening skills to the peace-making and reconciliation processes. An example of this is the Compassionate Listening Project that seeks to further understanding and healing between Palestinians and Israelis (www.compassionatelistening.org).

- *Foster reconciliation and healing:* Finding reconciliation within ourselves or with others from whom we have been estranged can neither be sought nor coerced. There is something about the flow of forgiveness and the intention of reconciliation that is mystical and pervasively spiritual. Once this kind of healing has occurred, the individual or community is free to move into the future unburdened by the past. Individuals cannot be coerced into forgiveness of self or other. To insist upon premature forgiveness and reconciliation is to perpetuate injustice. Reconciliation takes great effort and commitment. When individuals encounter genuine reconciliation in specific relationships, they also learn increasing flexibility in other relationships. The potential is there to learn how to live one's life with a desire to share in the rich, full humanity of each person encountered.

> In 1999, the human rights office of the Catholic Archdiocese of Guatemala released a book describing the Recovery of Historical Memory Project (REMHI). Believing that the best way to prevent future violence of the kind that terrorized the citizens of Guatemala was the reconstruction of truth (accurate memory), Monsignor Juan Gerardi published the findings of the REMHI work that was done in Guatemala in local parishes and churches. Gerardi's forward included the following comments:

> This is a pastoral approach. It is working with the light of faith to discover the face of God, the presence of the Lord. In all of these events it is God who is speaking to us. We are called to reconciliation. Christ's mission is one of reconciliation. His presence calls us to be agents of reconciliation in this broken society and to try to place the victims and the perpetrators within the framework of justice. People have died for their beliefs. Killers were often used as instruments. Conversion is necessary, and it is up to us to open spaces to bring about that conversion. It is not enough simply to accept the facts. It is necessary to reflect on them and to recover lost values.

As one part of the path to reconciliation, Gerardi recognized the centrality of recovering the truth of what had happened, of breaking the silence that had held victims and perpetrators in captivity. Stating further, "To open ourselves to truth and to face our personal and collective reality are not options that can be accepted or rejected. They are indispensable requirements for all people and all societies that seek to humanize themselves and to be free. They make us face our most essential human condition: that we are sons and daughters of God, called on to participate in our Father's freedom".

In the conclusions of the REMHI report, the authors note essential acts of reconstruction that provide the pathway to further violence prevention:

– Economic or material, social and cultural reparations to partially compensate victims for their losses
– Humanitarian medical, psychological, social and legal readaption measures that include individual, family and community-centred therapeutic approaches to healing
– Truth-telling in the historical and collective memory of Guatemalan society. These materials must recognize the multilingual, pluricultural and oral, nonliterate traditions of Guatemala's national identities

> - Honouring the victims by public, symbolic commemorations, monuments and tributes
> - Exhumations of massacres and reburial in consecrated grounds
> - Religious denominations teaching the concepts of reconciliation, forgiveness and peace
> - Monitoring and preventing additional human-rights violations
> - Creating social sanctions against recurrence of repressive violence
> - Monitoring law enforcement in the government's oversight of the peace
> - Restoring traditional authority to historical Mayan communities
> - Demilitarization
> - Land reform measures
> - Supporting the exercise of personal freedoms.
>
> It is clear from the REMHI report that reconciliation is neither a sentimental regret nor a whitewash operation. Rather, religiously based reconciliation work is a muscular, well-defined response of the church in which compassion, mercy and justice demand truth-telling, restitution and social reforms as part of the reconciliation call of the church to its culture and society.

- *Nurture fellowship among diverse peoples:* While most of us live in the midst of great cultural diversity, many of us do not make lasting, intimate friendships across cultural dividing lines. Sharing a meal is a great place to start. Table fellowship provides an opportunity for intimate conversations to occur. Churches can make a vital contribution to breaking down barriers by encouraging shared meals.

> Anglican Bishop Peter Storey of South Africa toured the United States before the ending of apartheid. He talked about the decision of some white South African

> Christian churches to begin to serve inclusive communal meals inside church buildings. During the apartheid era these meals were illegal. Even so, these South African Christians used this opportunity to meet and befriend each other across colour lines. The intention of these churches was to participate in the non-violent dismantling of the rule of apartheid.

In a socially stratified society, individuals need occasions to encounter each other across dividing lines of culture, racial origins, gender, economic diversity and ethnicity. Churches, temples, mosques, synagogues and other houses of religious worship can take the lead in providing opportunities for individuals of many faith traditions to come together to learn from each other. Religious groups and ministerial associations can create days of shared prayer, community activities in which all religious groups can participate without compromising their essential religious beliefs.

> One example of diversity appreciation and fellowship took place at Goshen College, a Mennonite college in Indiana. During a course in cross-religious dialogue, a Jewish rabbi taught one week of classes. On Friday evening a meal was shared in a local Mennonite home, where the rabbi explained to the class Jewish beliefs about the Sabbath and its importance to Jewish families. The special foods of the evening provided the backdrop for learning to relate in table fellowship across Jewish and Christian faith lines. In addition, the class visited a nearby mosque for evening prayers. The Muslim Imam guided them in a conversation about appropriate behaviours and dress, as well as the basic tenets of Islamic faith.

Programmes such as the Fellowship of Reconciliation in Nyack, New York, continue to work for non-violent social change with religious people of many faiths. In recent years, a concerted effort has been made to bring Christians, Jews and Muslims into working relationships with each other around issues of religious prejudice and interfaith hostilities.

2. Share the benefits of peace and healthy relationship-building

Religious groups have a mandate to be proactive in educating the general public and community for increased peace-building. As part of their educational outreach plan church leaders can:

- *Define a theology of peace:* R.N. Brock and R.A. Parker offer these suggestions for defining a theology of peace. First, each religious group needs to examine itself and its history in order to determine where its practices contribute to a theology of violence. Second, each religious group can articulate a peace-building theology that speaks prophetically to the ongoing violence of its own culture.

> Glide Methodist Church in San Francisco has ministries to homeless individuals as well as to people living with AIDS and other incapacitating physical and social disorders. The liturgical richness of Sunday worship is fuelled by the ethnic and economic diversity of the community and by the church's commitment to social justice advocacy within one of the poorest and most blighted neighbourhoods of San Francisco, one of the wealthiest cities in California (www.glide.org).

Other examples of integrating peace theology with practice come from the indigenous peoples of the world who often have the most advanced spiritual teachings about peace. In the early part of the 20th century, the North American Hopi Nation elders authorized several young men to go out into the world of industrialized nations to teach the Hopi prophecy regarding the destructive path of war and violence. From this experience Thomas Banyacya became one of the most eloquent peace teachers of the 20th century. He urged people of all races, nationalities and ethnicities to forego the violence of nuclear warfare. He encouraged returning to a state of balance and harmony in living with other humans and embracing the sacredness of the natural world. It was his spiritual centredness that allowed Banyacya to be prophetic.

- *Educate for healthy relationships:* One of the places in which churches can work proactively to educate members of the community is to assist them in understanding family patterns of abuse and violence. An example of this type of education is premarital counselling, which most churches require before marriage. By discussing marital violence with the couple while examining their conflict resolution patterns, premarital counsellors can do several things. They can set in place the expectation that violence should not occur within intimate relationships. They can open the door to both partners for immediate conversations if violence does erupt. They can begin to establish supportive communities around each new relationship inside the religious community.

3. Train interfaith church leaders

Leaders of all faiths are under a moral mandate to build social and spiritual capacity to work with those who are "hurting". Church leaders can maximize their effectiveness for peace- and relationship-building by convening their interfaith colleagues in partnerships around professional training. To best address this responsibility religious leaders can:

- *Explore violence perpetrated by clergy:* Regardless of the faith, religious leaders are increasingly faced with the issue of preserving relationship appropriateness with parishioners. Faith groups need to assure their leaders are carefully selected and well trained in pastoral care. Accountability structures are essential in order to assure the safety of all who seek assistance from pastoral care providers.
- *Educate for self-care for spiritual caregivers:* Any professional group who deals with the healing of others can itself become vulnerable and weary. Religious leaders and nurturers can utilize interfaith resources to help in training themselves and their staff for better methods of self-care and relationship building. A community that

offers spiritual retreats for religious leaders and others who work at healing the wounds of violence will promote the self-care needed in order to work at building a culture of peace.

4. Network across interfaith and secular community resources

Involving and networking with the entire community is important for community wide strategies to work. Church leaders can:

- *Focus on common mission:* Increasingly, faith-based groups work together for common, pro-social and peace-building efforts. It is relatively easy for individuals of diverse religious persuasions to come together around issues that affect the well-being of members of the community at large. Interfaith groups, mission-oriented and faith-motivated leaders and volunteers can work together at local, regional, national and international levels. Collaborative projects can make a significant impact on community spiritual, relational and social well-being.

> In southwest Michigan, the Stronger Together programme models the benefit of working together. Each week women from multiple faith communities and faith traditions meet to plan and address ways in which they can cooperate to reduce levels of family violence in Berrien County. While the group is not formally organized, these women collectively generate funds and educational visibility for the cause of reducing both child and spouse abuse. Some of the programme participants are themselves recovering victims. Others are mental health professionals from a variety of congregational backgrounds. Still others are lay volunteers who opt to do childcare and "safe-sheltering" for victims.
>
> Motivated by a sense of mission to build peaceful communities by helping troubled families, these

> women from diverse faith groups work collaboratively to improve the well-being of those who are being hurt by family and societal violence. The impact these women have had in the community prompted United Way to offer funding for their services to victims and victims' families. The group opted to turn down the opportunity for United Way funding because they wanted their own church institutions to provide funding to maintain this ministry. The women were collectively concerned that if and when funding came from outside the congregational pool, they could lose some of the faith communities' ownership of the programme. For them it is clear their services are effective because the congregations from which they come take ownership in providing the services.

5. Advocate congregational policies that promote a culture of peace

Faith groups can corporately and proactively endorse policies based on the religious principles of equity, fair play, full inclusion, appreciation of diversity and a sense of joy.

Religious institutions often lag behind their secular counterparts in creating honest and honourable work relationships for their own employees. Both religious lay leaders and ordained leaders need to be taught that a just institution is essential to carrying out a ministry of peace in the world. Proper procedures and protocols for supervising the religious institution's work in the world are essential. To achieve this goal, church leaders can:

- *Establish high ethical standards of personal conduct:* Faith institutions, as historical leaders, can operate as beacons of light or as havens of darkness. Recent scandals regarding particular behaviours of church leaders have caused great concern for accountability. Accountability needs to be guided by an unquestionable moral and ethical code. This code must be coupled with procedures that are based on the religious principles of equity, fair play and full inclusion. Faith institutions can provide support and assistance to religious leaders in order for them to acknowledge their own weaknesses and humanness and find ways to work within their own vulnerabilities.

For example, in the specific area of sexual abuse of lay members by members of the religious hierarchy, several denominations have now established protocols for handling such violations. In this situation, the rights of victims and the rights of the accused must both be addressed by proactive and honourable church policy. Creating a safe environment of openness to talking about sexuality is important. Safety to talk about these issues may encourage victims of sexual abuse to speak about their experience and get the assistance they need to heal. Explicitly communicating appropriate behaviours and expectations for clergy also helps prevent people from becoming victims.

- *Advance socially responsible priorities and policies:* Not only can faith institutions meet the spiritual needs of people, but they also have a spiritual and moral mandate to meet the physical and social needs of those in the community. Those houses of worship that have adopted open systems for serving in their communities are themselves blessed. Volunteerism can offer an increased sense of social and spiritual vitality. Faith-based communities where outreach and service are foundational can lead to increased faith-in-action participation from group members. Peace-building activities must be built upon strong community-church ties. Faith institutions that "walk the talk" of inclusiveness, tolerance and selfless service are laying the building blocks for a peace-filled community.

> West Central Neighbourhood Ministry, in Fort Wayne, Indiana, USA, is an ecumenical social service organization that enjoys strong interfaith support. Their goal is building a stronger, healthier Fort Wayne community. It began over 36 years ago with an effort on the part of the downtown churches to meet the needs of person's living within the shadows of their steeples.

> The current West Central programmes and activities include those for children and teens, older adults and entire families, as well as a food bank and extensive information and referral services. Five core values of respect, responsibility, truthfulness, trustworthiness and forgiveness provide the framework for these programmes. Annually, 2900 individuals are served through the centre programmes and services with 26,000 client contacts a year. Currently, 17 congregations have an active role in the work of West Central Neighbourhood Ministry. These represent twelve Christian denominations, including all three historic peace churches, and a Reform Jewish congregation.

While religious groups differ in social consciousness, many members now prefer that their faith institutions operate as venues for progressive social modelling. Parents encourage their children to be involved in practical community service activities, and they can offer a good example by volunteering themselves. Faith groups that offer opportunity for volunteerism often find an increase in charitable giving. When religious institutions demonstrate that they bring healing and hope to their communities, their membership increases.

6. Develop effective dialogue and lobbying strategies with local, regional and national legislative offices

Religious groups also need to work at influencing governmental and legislative changes that promote a culture of peace. In influencing dialogue and legislative process faith groups can:

- *Partner with local, regional and national governments for peace-building initiatives:* Much more can be achieved when governmental agencies partner with faith groups for social-change events. For example, in Goshen, Indiana, local churches came together to organize an alternative event in a local park when the Ku Klux Klan was given permission to gather at the local courthouse. To accomplish this alternative gathering, churches worked with the mayor's office as well as with the office of the chief of police. This event was so successful it is now an annual Day of Diversity event hosted by the Human Relations Council of the city. While individuals of faith continue to be involved in the planning, the city is the sponsor.

- *Mobilize religious leaders' moral authority:* Religious leaders can use the moral authority of their position to teach and inform. Some leaders themselves have witnessed the destructive power of violence in human life. They can offer a powerful voice for non-violent means of solving interpersonal and international conflicts.

> One religious leader offers an ideal model. Exiled during the Chinese take over of his homeland of Tibet, the current Dalai Lama is relentless in his teachings about spiritual peace and international peace as originating in the same spiritual source. He remains a powerful influence. All who know him comment on his infectious joy and playful spirit. The spirit of bitterness and hatred towards China is missing even as he advocates for justice for Tibet's remaining Buddhist culture.

- *Implement social activist initiatives:* Formal and informal religious groups can participate in basic efforts that promote significant long-term social change. Utilizing the Internet and other electronic technologies, the religious community can encourage large numbers of individuals to participate in community or nationwide peace actions.

> To impact legislative outcomes some faith-based groups have effectively used the following strategies and social action tools:
>
> – letter-writing campaigns
> – phone campaigns
> – electronic mail campaigns
> – street theater

- prayer vigils in public places of high visibility
- specific, well-organized, "mail-in" options such as the "no blood for oil" campaign of the Persian Gulf war in which film cartridges were labelled and sent to the White House mail room; or the "God asks us to feed our enemies, not bomb them" campaign before the USA bombing of Iraq in which small bags of white rice were sent to the White House mail room
- personal contacts and visits to legislator's offices either in the local area or at the state or national level
- testimonies and story-telling
- press conferences and press releases to local, regional or national media
- sit-ins and protest marches
- mobilization of public opinion through newspaper advertisements such as the ones published in the *New York Times* and other local newspapers during the protest before the beginning of the second Gulf war
- writing letters to the editor of local, regional or national newspapers
- utilizing multiple posters and distributing leaflets around a local area about a local issue
- well-publicized hunger fast
- in the United States, having a silent protest at the local post office on tax day (15 April) raises awareness for how much of the tax dollar goes to pay for past, present or future wars

Reflective questions
- How have you seen religion contribute to violence in your community?
- Where have you seen religion be effective in its peace-building work in your community and in the world?
- Where have you seen religious teaching help individuals to forgive one another and to reconcile with each other?

- How do churches foster individual attitudes for spiritual unity, reconciliation and peace-building?
- Can you suggest ways faith groups can educate themselves and their communities for increased acceptance of diversity?
- What ideas do you have for developing family-centred, peace-building programmes at your house of worship?
- What are some strategies faith groups could use to advocate for socially proactive organizational policies?
- What are some ideas for networking those of diverse faith traditions around community peace efforts?

5. The Media: Message Bearers for Peace-Building

"Love, love, Belize is...love!" How can a whole country be blanketed with a message of love? This message paints the colour of love as love for country, nature, diversity, children and democracy. The name of the national radio station in this small Central American country is Love FM, the theme for political campaigns is love, and heart-shaped blue signs are posted on light poles countrywide. Seaside towns, Mayan villages, urban centres – all are covered with the theme of love. Belizeans sing and dance about love. Every holiday stresses celebrating the spirit of love! The message is clear; even the youngest child can sing songs of Belizean love!

Groups and governments of questionable ethics often use the media to spread messages of violence and hatred. How much better would it be to use the media to nurture and foster messages of love, peace and safety! Belize's culture of love demonstrates that when all systems work together, utilizing the media as message bearers, change can happen.

Introduction

While there is overwhelming evidence that media violence predisposes people to violent attitudes and behaviours, the positive educational possibilities inherent in the media are endless. Given the right incentive, the entertainment industry could provide models for peace, non-violent conflict resolution and compassion. In addition, television news broadcasts could help build a culture of peace by producing more thoughtful analysis of issues that deal with the complexity and interconnectedness of problems

Constant exposure to media violence desensitizes children and adults to violence, teaching them to accept it as normal and essential for survival. In every nation, region or city, when television is introduced there is an immediate explosion of violence on the playground, and within 15 years the murder rate doubles.

Television violence by itself does not kill people. It destroys our violence "immune system" and conditions us to derive pleasure from violence. Violence is a staple of our mass media. The average American child spends thirty hours a week in front of the television set. Researchers George Comstock and Erica Scharrer report that children's programming is much more violent than general audience prime-time programming, and also that four out of five federal fact-finding task forces have concluded that media violence could be problematic in regard to the behaviour of the viewer.

We know from hundreds of studies that films, TV and video games play a role in furthering and reinforcing violence and create an atmosphere in which violence is normalized. Our children are becoming desensitized to violence because it is so pervasive in our media. We must educate our children and ourselves to think critically about the images that bombard them. We need to be able to deconstruct the powerful messages we receive to lessen their effect.

The media take many forms. Print media include newspapers, magazines, billboards, t-shirts, coffee mugs and even the church bulletin! Pervasive electronic media include radio, television, movies, video and computer games. While the media may be part of the problem of our violent culture, they also have the potential to be part of the solution for promoting a culture of peace.

The strengths-based peace-building actions recommended for the media and highlighted in this chapter are the following.

1. Offer programming that models peace-building behaviours

The media can be pressured to offer peace-promoting programming for individuals and their families. It is important that the entertainment and media industry recognize its social responsibility. A number of studies suggest that pro-social messages on television can have a greater effect on behaviour than anti-social messages. A media campaign can focus on the excitement of peace-building. Peace-building can be as entertaining as violence. Some approaches include:
- *Targeting children's programming:* Children are impressionable. The entertainment industry can help to

change stereotypes and prejudices, even those received from parents or friends.

> Channel Four in Northern Ireland began a television series for primary school aged children called *Sarah and the Whammi*. The impetus for this programme came out of a University of Ulster research project that showed that children were showing sectarian tendencies by the ages of three or four and that these dramatically increased by age six. To help counteract this biased socialization, the programme sought to teach children about:
> - human interdependence
> - respect for diverse cultural traditions
> - understanding conflict
> - dealing creatively with conflict
> - respect for self and others
> - building relationships
>
> By utilizing lovable characters and a creative storyline, the producers successfully created a popular television programme that advances acceptance of diversity in a highly polarized society. The programme teaches children to deal with their problems through story and their own fantasy world.

- *Realizing that people learn in different ways:* Some people learn best by hearing. Others learn best by seeing and touching. While the previous Northern Ireland example utilized the visual advantage of television, radio can also be effective in getting the message across.

> KMEL, a radio station in San Francisco, sponsors "Street Soldiers," a radio talk show that encourages young people to call in and talk about the realities of life in the inner city. This is an effort to encourage youth to express their anger, fear and frustration about the violence they experience in a way that gives them voice in the community while also finding sympa-

> thetic listeners. The programme host often gives advice and encouragement, offering alternatives to violence. The show also offers links to community programmes, services and resources. More details about this programme can be found in the book *Peace by Piece*.

2. Enhance media messages to educate for peace

The media and entertainment industry is uniquely positioned to educate the public and promote peace in powerful ways.

- *Design media blitzes:* Well-planned media blitzes can be a valuable tool in a plan to build peace in the community. These educational blitzes can be conducted at a local, regional or national level. Common examples include the anti-smoking and anti-drug public service announcements in the United States. Another simple ten-second public service message used by a local television station in the United States says: "Parents, it is ten o'clock. Do you know where your children are?"
- *Promote media literacy:* The pervasiveness and sophistication of media require us to be alert and savvy consumers. Bill Walsh, AV/Media specialist at Billerica high school in Massachusetts, which has a comprehensive media literacy programme, concludes that "television changes how we look at the world... It changes how we see things, what we think is important, what we think is normal and abnormal, and even whether our own lives are important or valuable or fulfilling".

3. Facilitate self-critical dialogue among media service providers

Members of the media can maximize their impact for peace-building by facilitating self-critical dialogue with their colleagues across the industry. To achieve this goal media representatives can be encouraged to:

- *Facilitate reflective dialogue:* S. Bloom and M. Reichert report that by age 18, the typical American child who watches 28 hours of television a week will have witnessed 40,000 simulated murders and 200,000 acts of violence. Viewing television programmes with a preponderance of violence has a profound effect on how children see the world and what they think is "normal". These programmes teach that violence is not only acceptable, it is the preferred way to solve problems. The entertainment industry must be persuaded by government or consumer actions such as boycotts to clean up the airwaves for our families and children.

4. Collaborate with other vital community partners

Media and entertainment industry leaders can be encouraged to network with other important partners in order to:

- *Voice the message:* Media professionals have literally compelling voices for sharing community visions for community wide peace-building. As highly visible leaders, TV and radio personalities are part of the community. They can take community service messages to schools, malls, churches and special events.

> An anti-violence event in a northern Indiana community engaged a well-known local television news broadcaster as the emcee [master of ceremonies] for the event. His popularity helped bring people to the event. His involvement also benefited the television station by promoting their image as being involved in the community and supporting violence prevention efforts.

- *Facilitate community partnership:* Media entities are uniquely positioned to invite businesses, community and public service agencies to rally around peace-building. As visible leaders, media representatives can mobilize their communication resources to motivate key players to help build a culture of peace. After the school shootings at Columbine, a local television station in Indiana hosted a town hall meeting, inviting local experts to address the issue of school violence, taking questions and comments from the audience. This meeting was televized live and highlighted on the evening news broadcast. This is a good example of news media taking the initiative to engage the community in dialogue around important issues that affect everyone. While in this example it took a serious violent crime to initiate a conversation, what would happen if a community took seriously the idea to build a culture of peace and hosted town hall meetings around the theme of creating peace instead of waiting for a disaster to occur?

5. Develop ethical guidelines and policies for presenting peace-friendly products

Media organizations can be urged to make policy and establish procedures that ensure ethical responsibility. This kind of self-monitoring activity could include:

- *Ensuring socially responsible profit-making:* Success in television programming is not based on the content of the programming, nor on the quality of the programming, but rather on the size of the audience it sells to advertisers. Violence seems to sell, and commercials are increasingly violent. To counter this influence in the United States, the Public Broadcasting Service (PBS) raises operational funds from its viewers and does not rely on promoting products or services for its income. During a recent fund-raising campaign, PBS emphasized its commitment to non-violent programming.

> In Indiana an anti-smoking campaign is currently being promoted by an organization called White Lies. To counter the tobacco industry marketing of their product to children, the White Lies campaign produces thought-provoking 30-second public service announcements that local television stations can use to promote healthful living. They use catchy tunes or sayings that are easy to remember. Their purpose is to help children choose not to begin to smoke. For more information, check their website at www.whitelies.tv.

Religious groups or discussion groups can arrange a showing of films like "Killing Us Softly", an examination of how advertising exploits women, or of "Tough Guise", an examination of how the media portrayal of men shapes their notions of masculinity.

- *Emphasize balanced news reporting:* It is important that all forms of media report "good" news rather than concentrating their primary coverage on one disaster after another. Often the media present oversimplified and unbalanced news coverage. Instead they could provide a service to the public by modelling how to think about, discuss and resolve more complicated and multidimensional issues. News anchor-persons could articulate a new ethical commitment to show good news and features in addition to the daily dose of disaster coverage. A beginning is to commit to one violence-free hour of news and programming every day.

> In a local newspaper, an entire column in the sport section was devoted to reporting the school board's decision to hire a track coach for the local high school. Paragraphs were written about this person's accomplishments in track and field events, while one short sentence indicated that he would be teaching biology. Why? Did the school board hire a teacher or a coach? Why are our teachers not given as many accolades as our coaches?
>
> Every newspaper and television newscast has an entire section devoted to sports. Imagine what would happen if equal time and attention were given to education. Imagine an entire section of the daily news devoted to reporting on the good things happening in the schools, providing news clippings of teachers doing their jobs in creative and effective ways. Imagine having the daily news reporting on the latest research in education, on how children best learn and the most effective teaching methods.

> The news media can lead the way in creating a culture whereby education is valued as much or more than sports. What impact would this have on the community?

6. Promote critical responses to the media

- *Promote new parental media guidelines:* Consumers and other groups can promote the recommendations of the American Medical Association's *Physicians Guide to Media Violence* as found in S. Bloom and M. Reichert:
- be aware of the shows your children watch
- avoid using television, videos or video games as babysitters
- limit the use of media – no more than one to two quality hours per day with none before school, during the daytime hours, during meals or before homework is done
- turn the television off during meal times
- keep televisions and video players out of children's bedrooms
- decide in advance if a programme is worth viewing and turn on the television only when there is something specific you have decided is worth watching
- don't make the TV the focal point of the house
- watch what your children are watching and discuss with them what they are seeing
- be especially careful of viewing just before bedtime
- establish explicit guidelines for appropriate movie viewing and review proposed movie choices in advance
- become "media literate"; learn how to evaluate media offerings critically; teach your children about the influence of advertising
- set a good example for your children by limiting your television viewing
- let your voice be heard; write to or call advertisers; insist on better programming for our children.

One example of effective public pressure involved the removal of Howard Stern's radio programme, considered highly offensive by many members of the American public, from the roster of Clear Channel Communications. The media giant also paid a substantial fine to the Federal Communication Commission.

Reflective questions
- What critical strategies can the media use for exploring the impact of their current programming?
- How can the media promote peace with their programming?
- Can you suggest ethical guidelines and policies that the media could develop for presenting peace-friendly products?
- Why is it important for the media to promote a safe environment through factual and timely reporting?
- How can you influence your local television stations to promote programming that promotes a culture of peace?
- Since media are businesses, bent on profit-making, how can they be motivated to change what seems to be working well?

6. Community Organizations and the Public Sector

The city of Salinas, located about two hours south of San Francisco in Monterey County, USA, is known as the salad bowl of the country. Migrant farm workers provide most of the labour for this agricultural economy.

In a collaborative planning process with the Prevention Institute (Berkeley, California), the city, along with community leaders, developed a framework of effective strategies for violence prevention. Their vision was one of community compassion, respect and responsibility. Their plan developed over a four-month period with a core group of twenty people meeting six times for four to five hours each time. They consulted a network of one hundred community leaders who met with them three times.

The groups identified several risk factors of particular concern to Salinas including high truancy rates, low literacy rates, lack of affordable housing, and overcrowded schools and neighbourhoods.

A successful approach to promoting peace must include building on positive resources that help the community become resilient, resist violence and counteract risk factors. The plan to cultivate peace in Salinas was built upon a wide range of resources by coordinating multiple efforts in a strategic and deliberate way.

The coalition's strategy included a long-term focus on outcomes; changing people, norms and policies; and collaborative initiatives and partnerships across disciplines. Funding for the planning process came from several foundations as well as the city budget. A large federal grant provided funding for the programmes put in place by the planning process. When asked what would happen when the grant funding expired, the mayor said, "If cities can pass a tax referendum to build large sports arenas, why can't they pass a referendum to pay for activities that create peaceful community?"

Introduction

A discussion about the public sector is by nature quite broad, including representatives of the criminal justice system, law enforcement, and local government (city, town, county). These are the people who occupy positions of influence. Their approach to community well-being can determine the success or failure of building a culture of peace. It is important to include them in planning and delivery of programmes that reduce violence and build peace in our homes, schools and neighbourhoods.

Among the strengths-based peace-building actions recommended for the public sector and highlighted in this chapter are the following.

1. Providing public sector programmes that promote a culture of peace for individuals and families

Developing the peace-making skills of individuals involves creating governmental, social service and public-sector programming that nurtures a sense of peace and safety for individuals and families.

- *Programme for safety:* Involving all the local partners – schools, parks, human-relations commissions, social-service providers – in planning opportunities for individual participation in peace-building events is of utmost importance. In blighted sections of towns and cities, resources for mural painting in strategic places with supervision by the parks department and artistic assistance from local art teachers or the local art league can be provided. Philadelphia, Pennsylvania and Belfast, Northern Ireland, are examples of cities where murals have become tourist attractions.

The town council can organize monthly "safe nights" an opportunity for youth to congregate to socialize, dance, participate in fun, healthy activities and learn about positive peer interaction and conflict resolution through a planned activity during the evening. Space can be provided by the local park or school. One example from the city of Salinas, California, implemented after a collaborative review of their community appears below.

> The Safe Teens Empowerment Project (STEPS) is a teen programme that trains youth in self-motivation,

> how to talk to the media about issues important to youth, anger management and self-esteem. Teens work with the police on alcohol issues, sometimes acting as undercover agents to see if the liquor store will sell alcohol to them. A teen coalition meets monthly to provide inspirational speakers and other positive alternatives for evening activities. Youth enjoy being involved in this programme as it gives them a sense of being able to do something to improve their community while developing their own skills.

2. Focusing on community-wide peace education

The purpose of community education is to provide information to the general public, generally disseminated by government agencies and public sector service providers.

- *Educate via one-to-one relationship building:* Bike rodeos hosted by police officers are a good way to both teach safety skills and allow children to have a good time while becoming better acquainted with their local police officer. The recent trend towards community policing also promotes relationship building. Programmes that encourage police officers to buy homes in their community of jurisdiction also promote relationship building.
- *Educate via social events:* Other community education efforts that can build a culture of peace include annual ethnic festivals and celebration of diversity days in which community members come together to organize and sponsor a day of discovery and celebrating the differences within the community. Food, drama, song and dance, poetry and story-telling, and arts and crafts are well received and provide not only an opportunity for healthy engagement of both youth and adults in an enjoyable activity, but also offer an opportunity to gain appreciation for other cultures within the community.
- *Educate via the media:* Collaborating with the media to get out the message is an important and necessary component to the success of any programme. Billboards and radio spots can raise community awareness of availability

of the social services while also recognizing the need for such services. In addition, mass media campaigns are a great way to get out the message of peace and good will. Blanketing a community with a peacefulness campaign promotes the idea that "violence is not the way we do things here" and that "peace is for everyone here". (Remember the example from Belize in chapter 5?)

3. Nurturing human resources that promote peace

The public sector is responsible for educating staff and community leaders about peace-building skills. Ideas of how to do this include:

- *Train public servants:* The public sector can advance peace-building and mediation skills among governmental and public sector employees. Police officers can be trained in conflict resolution and anger management skills to use in de-escalating tense situations. Mediation services should be available and their use encouraged. Community workers can use mediation to handle neighbourhood disputes. Providing continuing education in these areas is important as it keeps the skills sharp and provides up-to-date information and techniques for those on the frontline of violence prevention and peace-building.

4. Fostering collaboration, participation and network development

It is important to build community peace-building strategies from the ground up. Without broad collaborative partnerships between citizens, public sector service providers and social service agencies, there is little or no likelihood that change will be sustainable. Peace-building includes community-wide networking and collaboration. Community-based organizations are most effective when they choose to:

- *Foster interagency collaboration:* P.W. Mattessich, M. Murray-Close and B.R. Monsey define collaboration as a mutually beneficial and well-defined relationship entered

into by two or more organizations to achieve common goals. The relationship includes a commitment to mutual and egalitarian relationships and goals, a jointly developed structure with shared responsibility, mutual authority and accountability for success, as well as sharing resources and rewards.
- *Partner with the grassroots:* Not only do organizations need to collaborate with each other to address the needs of the community; they also need to meet and work with individuals most affected by violence in our culture. Providing opportunities for becoming acquainted with one another through neighbourhood barbeques, open houses and ethnic fairs that celebrate diversity are several ways to involve individuals in building a culture of peace.
- *Mobilize community leadership:* Finding and empowering impassioned leaders to mobilize grassroots networks is the secret to energizing any public change initiative. Finding these leaders is done by asking a few key questions: "Who are the people in the community that know the most about the issue at hand? Who cares the most about making the changes needed to reduce violence in the community? Who has the resources needed to contribute to the project?" Projects designed with the people most affected by violence are the most likely to succeed.
- *Establish routine neighbourhood dialogues:* No one knows better the problems of a neighbourhood or town than the people who live there. Local neighbourhood meetings in which residents are free to express their opinions about the problems and strengths of their neighbourhoods go a long way to creating social policies that benefit everyone.
- *Monitor and coordinate community-wide service provision:* Leaders of the public sector can bring community groups together to ensure provision of services and to eliminate duplications. Law enforcement personnel are in a unique position to assure those in need find the resources available in the community. Every police car can be equipped with a current referral list for various

community agencies, complete with contact names and phone numbers.
- *Enlist broad-based community resources:* Ensuring peace-building success requires having as many of the community resources involved as possible. For example, local law-enforcement agencies or town councils may want to enlist the aid of a local college or university to assist in preparing data collection or for expertise in designing a research project to ascertain the efficacy of various prevention programmes. Utilizing this resource would give them good quantitative and qualitative demographic data on which to base programmatic decisions and raise funds (see ch. 7).

5. Revising governmental programme policies and practices for promoting a culture of peace

Institutions, public and private, can change their practices to ensure successful peace-building outcomes. Because of the complex nature of their work, it is sometimes hard to convince members of the public sector to seek strengths-based initiatives when they are used to reacting to an immediate crisis. Because these institutions are responsible for the safety of the community, at times reaction is necessary. However, it is dangerous to be constantly in the urgent mode. We recommend that, like Salinas, community leaders call together people from both private and public sectors to examine their community and prepare a plan to build the peace of the community.

- *Link values to policy change proposals:* If it is true that a community's (or nation's) values are reflected in how it spends its money, then we need to take a closer look at our budgets. For example, in the US, former admirals, generals and military officials agree that the Pentagon budget could safely be reduced by 15 percent (based on 2003 figures). That's enough to do *all* of the following:
- Provide basic health and food to the world's poor: $12 billion

- Rebuild America's public schools over 10 years: $12 billion
- Reduce class size for grades 1-3 to 15 students per class: $11 billion
- Reduce debts of impoverished nations: $10 billion
- Provide health insurance to all uninsured American children: $6 billion
- Increase federal funding for clean energy and energy efficiency: $6 billion
- Provide public financing for all federal elections: $1 billion
- Fully fund the US children's programme Head Start: $2 billion.

Priorities for how to spend the nation's resources can be made to enhance the life of the populace and reduce poverty. This will require tireless effort from individuals in both the public and the private sector.

- *Ask difficult questions:* The questions the public sector and community members need to ask are, "What causes people to offend and break the law? Has our education system failed them? Are they not equipped with the skills needed to get a job? Are there not jobs available for them? What are the barriers that prevent people from reaching their full potential? Why is drug trafficking attractive? Does it have to do with not being able to make ends meet at a minimum wage job?"

In the United States, a single mother with one child needs to work 100 hours a week at minimum wage to make ends meet. In the movie *Bowling for Columbine*, producer-director Michael Moore presents an example from Flint, Michigan, of a six-year-old who shot and killed a classmate using a gun he found at his uncle's house. He and his mother had recently moved in with the uncle when the mother was evicted from her apartment because she could not afford to pay the rent. The child was unsupervised because his mother was absent from home from before dawn until late at night working two jobs trying to earn enough money to meet their basic living expenses. The hard question in this case is, "Does our community have the will to assure adequate housing and supervision for all its children?"

- *Place emphasis on making proactive changes:* Those in decision-making positions need to think in more creative, proactive ways. A local county council in northern Indiana decided to raise property taxes in order to have available $68 million over a ten-year period for building and expanding correctional facilities. Where do we want to put our resources? Sixty-eight million dollars can buy a multitude of prevention services that could significantly reduce the need for more space in juvenile detention centre and adult prisons. More positive and productive uses of resources include:

- job training for the unemployed and under-educated
- transportation to jobs – access to work day or night
- child-care – day, evening and night shifts
- after-school programming, including summer, with an emphasis on the arts
- affordable and accessible health care
- education for all children of the community
- conflict resolution and bully prevention programmes
- drug rehabilitation programmes
- youth development programmes – leadership, conflict resolution
- safe places to congregate
- mediation services to reconcile relationships
- therapeutic services for victims of violence
- alternatives to incarceration so that low-risk female offenders can stay home with their children, and low-risk males can be with their families.

6. Advocating for pro-peace legislation and funding priorities

Significant for peace-building initiatives is the degree to which funding priorities funnel resources to social action programmes such as those listed above. It is discouraging that governments are willing to spend vast resources on punitive measures, yet little or no fiscal resources are available for prevention programme funding. To be truly effective, social service providers and community-based organizations can use their credibility in and knowledge of the community to work at influencing governmental legislation, including establishing funding priorities. To build a culture of peace, the public sector needs to think in new ways by:

- *Listening to the voices and ideas of victims of violence:* Victims of physical or more subtle forms of structural violence can be encouraged to share their experiences with people in power along with their ideas for prevention programmes. When peace-builders attempt to influence governments, they become advocates. Victims, accompanied by advocates, are a powerful voice in persuading legislatures of the need for change.

> Michael MacDonald was raised in a public housing project of South Boston. Violence had a great impact on his life as he witnessed his mother hit by a stray bullet and lost his siblings to personal and community violence. As a way of managing his grief and rage, Michael became active in organizing South Boston's gun buy-back programme. In four years, nearly three thousand guns were collected and destroyed.

- *Be strategic and creative:* Offer well conceptualized plans and anticipate the final outcome. Draft a model for what you are proposing. When suggesting policy changes, think "outside the box". Are there examples of ideas and strategies that work? If so, use them. Change is difficult for individuals and even more so for government entities. Keep written records of meetings, keep orderly files of letters written to and received from government agencies, and follow up meetings with a memo summarizing the conversation including any agreements made. Advocating for legislative changes requires collaborating with community partners and utilizing the media to take your message to the public.

- *Use your contacts:* Good use of relationships is vital. Use your networking and relationships in the community to help get meetings with key officials in places of power.
- *Take baby steps:* Social activists who are rigid and outspoken often make little headway when it comes to "selling" their product. Often repressive societies or settings will consider making small changes, but outwardly they reject the notion of radical change. Successful social action must be open to negotiation. Often change will be slow and incremental, but it will happen.
- *Build a critical mass:* Participatory change methods need the backing of a significant group able to build up a critical mass. This critical mass needs to represent a diverse constituency. Collaborative effort is far more effective than working alone.
- *Quantifying impact comparisons:* Numerical data and comparative analysis is typically a good tool to use for educating public servants. The media have routinely used this strategy for lobbying and building awareness. For example, when the local newspaper ran the story about the county officials deciding to build a correctional facility, the story next to it was about how difficult it is for working families to make ends meet. "A family of "two adults, a toddler and a school-age child needs at least $36,115 per year according to the Indiana Coalition on Housing and Homeless Issues in a report about self-sufficiency in Indiana counties." The self-sufficiency standard is how much a family needs to earn to get along without public or private assistance. It is interesting that these stories were juxtaposed because they are inextricably connected. Our values are reflected by how we choose to spend our money. It appears that this community sets its priorities on reactive measures such as building prisons rather than assuring that young children are adequately housed, fed and educated.
- *Present fiscal alternatives:* It is important to demonstrate how alternative funding patterns could impact long-term outcomes. For example, simply put, the juvenile justice

system and the prisons are full and overflowing because we are failing to provide the prevention services necessary to ensure that our youth and adults make good behaviour choices. It is crucial to ask, "Why are our prisons overflowing?" and "Why are there so many youth in need of services at the juvenile justice facility?"

Currently, our public sector spends most of its energy and resources on reacting to problems. Most programmes are designed to repair the proverbial leaky roof. We are suggesting here that instead of finding new and creative ways to repair the leak, to think instead in terms of replacing the whole roof.

Reflective questions
- How can you encourage participation of grassroots citizens in community projects?
- What can you do to ensure that current public sector activities and programmes are proactive?
- What can be done to ensure that all systems of government are collaborating and networking?
- What are some bipartisan strategies that could promote peace-building in your community?
- How can these activities be funded?

7. If You Want Peace, Work for Justice

Building peace in one's community requires working together for the common good. It is important to think in terms of working across disciplines and from the micro to the macro level. While we have already talked about what each sector of society could do at various levels, it is important also to understand the importance of working across sectors. To be most effective requires collaboration of all sectors of the community with someone taking the lead – for instance a municipal office, such as the example of Salinas, or a church or social service agency, to assemble a team of community peace-builders. Here are some ways to invite collaboration:

- *List assets:* At the outset of any social action project it is important to assess community needs and find, evaluate and organize all the resources available to assist in meeting the project goals. Often students in community action projects are eager to jump right into "difference-making" activities and forgo the time and expense of needs and resource assessment. But none of us would be happy about seeing a doctor for some physical malady if the doctor does not take the time to ask a few important questions that will assist him/her in understanding our condition. Surveying assets offers a natural way of looking at what is working in the community in order to design projects that mobilize community strengths. Often people do not realize the resources already available in the community. These resources can be used to build a culture of peace.

"Mapping" those assets can help. Mapping consists of identifying the community strengths by adapting the following checklist to ascertain the community talent and resources that can be used in a peace-building project. Enter each asset identified into a database or put names, addresses, and contact information on colour-coded index cards. Collect the information in a manner that is useful to communicate, solicit and document the response of each peace-building resource. Along with the contact information, note what each is willing to offer, as well as other pertinent facts. When you have compiled this list, plot all these resources on a map of your community.

> **Community-organizational asset checklist**
> *Community leaders:* known community leaders and project resource generators such as mayors, council persons, wealthy citizens
> *Other human resources:* those marginalized but who bring unique perspectives and resources to a project (i.e. elderly, teens, children, disabled)
> *Citizen groups:* associations or groups of citizens that function either formally or informally within a community, including youth groups
> *Local institutions:* social service organizations, churches, businesses, public service, and other non-profit and governmental agencies, schools, libraries
> *Physical assets:* land, building space, streets, transportation systems, soup kitchens, meeting rooms, parks and recreational facilities
> *Project leaders:* selected people who could take a leadership role and energize your project
> *Availability* of affordable housing, healthcare, employment, transportation

While this book emphasizes strengths-based activities, it may be helpful as you prepare an asset map to prepare a risk map as well. Utilizing a map of the community, plot the locations of known alcohol and drug outlets, gun shops, gang activity, closed businesses and industries, inadequate or at-risk schools and other pertinent information. On the same map, plot the assets of the community found during the asset survey. Also note where the majority of police calls occur.

You can get a quick understanding of the community by putting both the assets and the risks on the same map, quickly revealing the strengths of the community and where those strengths are most needed.

- *Use information wisely:* Surveying assets and risks can be a valuable tool to improve a community's ability to provide services. To build a culture of peace will require a working paradigm in which working collaboratively and sharing information is done willingly because it promotes the cause of peace-building in the community. And that is the ultimate goal. Never take your eyes off the prize! When you empower your collaborative partners with information, you can accomplish much good.

- *Promote healthy communication:* Healthy communication patterns are one key to success for those who agree to work together for the common goal of peace-building. Faulty communication and interpersonal behaviour patterns can include gossiping, blocking conversation about an issue that is perceived as threatening, group-think patterns in which thoughtful, helpful dissent is silenced, and agreeing just to be polite (rather than participating actively in change activities). Healthy communication, on the other hand, is open, honest, direct and shares needed information freely.

Conflict is especially important for working groups to manage. Verbal expressions of conflict (including conflicted feelings within the group) can be valuable to the group when they are used to foster inter-group understanding of complex issues. Healthy communication patterns require several essential skills:

- speaking in respectful and honest ways about one's own perceptions of the situation at hand
- compassionate listening (as neutral of judgment as possible) to another's opinions, beliefs and values
- making an interpersonal agreement, at times, to disagree respectfully
- negotiating significant differences among individuals or community groups until win-win solutions can be found

- *Generate human resources:* There are individuals and groups who are already making a contribution to peace-building or who have a rich potential to do so. Locating and empowering these human resources is important for community-based organizations that wish to be active in small- or large-scale peace-building activities. Without a committed group of people (whether volunteers or community organization leaders), little positive change will be accomplished. In general, peace-building activities will be most effective when they include both professionals and concerned citizens.

> In the United States, a small group of mothers, incensed by the growing numbers of children who were being killed in accidents involving drunken drivers, organized themselves into MADD (Mothers Against Drunk Driving). Twenty years later, many states and local communities have stricter law enforcement practices regarding drunk drivers. Many states require the drivers to attend classes. Some states have tightened their driver license requirements. The upward curve of child deaths has turned downward (www.madd.org/home/).

Questions that community change organizers need to ask themselves are, Who else needs to be at this table? What groups with a stake in this issue are either under-represented or not present at all? For any project to benefit from its investment of human capital, groups need to consider the following groups for representation in the planning process:
- *Young people:* Youth are always a source of enthusiasm and creativity. If one of the issues in a community is to stop youth violence from beginning or to create less of it, then young people must be involved in the planning. These youth need to reflect significant ethnic, religious, class and gender groups.
- *Senior citizens:* Elders with the wisdom of life can bring immense gifts of time, energy, and life-information to any working group. Among the Mennonites in Northern Indiana, some senior citizens have organized themselves into Seniors for Peace. This group organizes seminars on local and national peace concerns, participates in lobbying activities at a state and national level, helps fund

college student activities, prays together and works with local Mennonite congregations on peace and justice issues. Many of these individuals wear a blue tee-shirt that says "Senior for Peace" when attending a public event.

- *Musical, visual and theatrical artists:* The community of artists often creates visual and musical resources for peace. It is impossible to measure the effect of Joan Baez or Peter, Paul and Mary in creating the music of peaceful protests. Today a group calling themselves "The Raging Grannies" is putting protest words to popular tunes to be sung at anti-war rallies. Picasso's *Guernica* or Lehmbruck's *Fallen Warrior* or Kollwitz's *Seed Corn Shall Not Be Ground* or Augsburger's *Swords to Plowshares* sculpture all speak profoundly to the human spirit about violence and the need for peace. Shakespeare's *Hamlet* and *King Lear* instruct us in the powerful consequences of violence.
- *People with disabilities:* Physically and mentally challenged individuals are often overlooked resources for peace-building activities. Because they intimately know the realities of social structures they encounter every day, they have personal contributions to offer that no one else has. Visual artist Chad Friesen's work was chosen for a postcard used by United States peace activists (www.godseyeart.com).

• *Generate financial resources:* Beyond the vital need for human resources, all social action activities require financial resources. Fund-raising is not an easy art. Even with the best cause, acquiring funds to implement and sustain a project is difficult. Good funding plans include receiving monies from as many sources as possible. The ideal scenario includes obtaining one-third of the revenues from an annual campaign that includes donations from individuals and businesses. Another third should be generated from fee-for-service activities such as conducting training, paying clients, publications and in making available local experts to do consulting services. The final third (or less if possible) of the funding comes from outside grants and/or major corporate donations. There are many resources that can provide information on how to write grants for these monies. The Foundation Center (www.foundationcenter.org) has valuable information at their website. The Grantsmanship Center (www.tgci.com) provides a free subscription to its newsletter to not-for-profit agencies. It is imperative that peacemakers become savvy fund-raisers in order to build a culture of peace. Be creative and innovative in finding financial resources.

- *Ensure programme sustainability:* Develop a solid plan that ensures adequate funding long enough to make a difference. An evaluation plan needs to be in place from the beginning of the project in order to show financial providers they are not wasting their money.
- *Document programme outcomes:* Any peace-building effort that a social service agency or community-based organization develops is dedicated to making a difference in the lives of individuals and families. These outcomes are benefits or positive changes that affect the well-being of individuals or populations during or after participating in programme activities. Outcomes may relate to knowledge, attitudes, values, skills, behaviours, conditions or other attributes. For example, in a programme to reduce bullying behaviours among school children in an urban school, one desired outcome could be to reduce verbal threats in a given classroom environment as a way to improve social safety for all children.
- *Evaluation:* Assessing the overall effectiveness of projects should be done in several stages. Evaluation should be planned even before the project begins. The first stage is to clarify the outcome expectations, the second is to define the sources of data, the third is to plan data collection methods, the fourth is to arrange and monitor the integrity of the data collection, the fifth is to tabulate the data, and the final stage is to report the findings to key

players and the constituents of the service. Evaluation of peace-building efforts is extremely important.

No project can make a successful contribution to peace-filled living without a clear sense of mission, goals and objectives. Successful organizations will accomplish the following:

- *Define a mission:* A mission statement is a broad statement of purpose. Develop a mission statement that is brief, clear and appealing. This statement contains a succinct, appealing description of your organization or coalition and a summary of the goals and objectives you plan to accomplish.
- *Identify goals:* Goals are derived from the mission. They are broad and more encompassing. Goals are the building blocks upon which more specific objectives and activities can be based.
- *Delineate objectives:* Objectives offer measurable outcomes that are used to document the success of the peace-building effort. Generally, a good objective contains:
  - a results orientation, clearly stating the anticipated outcome to be achieved;
  - a measurable quantity permitting evaluation of the degree to which the goal has been achieved;
  - a time factor, specifying the time frame for achievement; and
  - an expression of achievability: the potential for actual attainment based on realistic assessment.
- *Bring it all together:* Just how effectively all these elements come together will determine the overall impact your project will have on peace-building. From asset mapping to project evaluation, each step is important to helping achieve the mission. Following is a fictional model of "Project X" that develops the framework for a peace-building initiative. Quantifiable achievements should be specified for each objective. The numbers below can and should be adjusted to community needs. The timeline for these goals and objectives is two to five years.

Project X: Mission, Goals and Objectives

MISSION: TO DEVELOP A CULTURE OF PEACE IN OUR COMMUNITY

Goal 1: Create affordable housing for a neighbourhood at risk
Objective 1: Explore federal grant programmes and foundation sources for low-income housing development.

Objective 2: Provide training and incentives for home ownership to 10 low-income head of households.

Objective 3: Organize 50 community volunteers to assist 10 low-income homeowners with home maintenance and repairs.

Goal 2: Encourage school attendance and job skill development
Objective 1: Work with the local public school on an alternative to suspension programme for 15 students.

Objective 2: Survey local industry to ascertain the skills needed by employees and determine if the schools are developing these skills in their students.

Objective 3: Explore local and regional funding opportunities for job skills training, as well as federal grants.

Objective 4: Develop a working group of 15 people from the local public school, college/university, unemployment agency and social service case managers to create incentives to keep students engaged in academic pursuits through college or vocational training.

Objective 5: Assist 3 high schools in providing the skills training needed by the local industry through school-to-work programmes.

Goal 3: Assure access to equal and equitable health care
Objective 1: Convene a meeting of 10 representatives from local health care providers (including mental health) to monitor the provision of health care services to all citizens.

Objective 2: Organize one health fair at the local mall with blood pressure screening, well-baby checks, and nutritional information.

Objective 3: Work with public schools to offer health clinics at the school every other week to provide immunizations, well-baby checks and other health services.

Objective 4: Organize a mobile dental programme in 5 elementary schools twice a year utilizing volunteer dentists and dental hygienists.

Goal 4: Assure access to employment
Objective 1: Explore funding for evening and night child care in addition to day care to ensure adequate supervision of children 24 hours a day.

Objective 2: Encourage 5 local industries to provide space for quality childcare centres site with provision of 24-hour services. Encourage scheduling employee breaks to coincide with mealtimes and bedtimes for the children so the parent can interact with the child during the break.

Objective 3: Provide (through city or county government) provision of low-cost transportation to and from work 24 hours a day for low-income people to be able to get to work whatever shift they happen to work.

Objective 4: Ensure quality supervision before and after school for children through middle school, including school holidays and breaks.

Objective 5: Provide an adult job-training programme that prepares people for employment in local industry.

Objective 6: Encourage family-centred standards in business that include parental leave benefits, time off to attend school functions etc.

Goal 5: Discourage local brain drain in the community
Objective 1: Provide 5 college scholarships for qualified individuals to develop job skills in the areas most needed in the community with the provision they must remain in (or return to) the community to live and work for a minimum of five years.

Objective 2: Provide 3 opportunities for cultural enrichment through community-wide events such as ethnic festivals, art shows and entertainment.

Goal 6: Provide enrichment opportunities for the youth
Objective 1: Work with the local artists guild to provide opportunities for involvement in drama, music (choral and instrumental), dance and art classes including drawing, painting and ceramics.

Objective 2: Organize three field trips to museums (art, history, science etc.), state and national parks, points of historical interest, local industries, organic farms etc.

Objective 3: Organize three special theme days at the local parks re: children's day, teen day, intergenerational play day – with activities geared to the age group.

Objective 4: Provide communication, conflict resolution, anger management, friendship and impulse control skill development opportunities at all youth events.

> *Goal 7: Create a marketing campaign for a culture of peace*
> Objective 1: Convene a working group of 15 representatives from local television, radio and print media to develop a marketing strategy for use in the community.
>
> Objective 2: Model the strategy on the "global coca-colanization" model.
>
> Objective 3: Utilize 5 local youth to prepare public service announcements for television, radio and the print media.
>
> *Goal 8: Promote ideas for self-sustaining community*
> Objective 1: Establish five community gardens.
>
> Objective 2: Teach organic gardening methods to ten people.

Reflective qestions
- Begin to survey your community by listing the organizational assets you have to use for peace-building. Then go out and walk your neighbourhood to find out more. What are they? Where are they located?
- What strategies can you use to promote healthy communication?
- Can you define your peace-building mission, goals and objectives?
- How do you propose to foster collaboration and network development?
- What ideas do you have for getting the resources needed to do your peace-project?
- What methods are you going to use to assess your outcomes?
- What specific ideas do you have to advocate for better peace-building legislation?

Appendix: Violence Prevention Spectrum

Prevention spectrum	Education Public schools and other educational institutions	Criminal justice/ Law enforcement/ Municipalities Courts, probation, police, city hall	Health Hospitals, health clinics, public health department, medical auxiliary	Community based organizations	Social service providers Community centres, department of family services etc.	Media TV, radio, newspapers bill boards etc.	Religious community	Youth
Individual knowledge & skill development								
Community education								
Provider training								
Coalition and network development								
Changing organizational practices								
Policy and legislation that supports prevention								

Source: Larry Cohen – Prevention Institute, Oakland California – For more information see www.preventioninstitute.org

References

The authors have used the following resource materials:

Chapter 1

Barash, D. and Webel, C. P. (2002). *Peace and Conflict Studies*. Thousand Oaks, CA, Sage Publications.

Brown, R. M. (1987). *Religion and Violence*. Philadelphia, Westminster.

Cohen, L. and Swift, S. (1999, September). "The Spectrum of Prevention", in *Injury Prevention 5*(3), pp.203-207.

Hanh, T. N. (1991). *Old Path, White Clouds*. Berkley CA, Parallax.

Hanh, T. N. (2002). *Peace Making*. Boulder CO, Sounds True.

Krug, E. G., Dahlberg, L. L., Mercy, J. A., Zwi and Lozano, R. (2002). *World Report on Violence and Health*. Geneva, World Health Organization.

McFadden, D. J. (2003, March). *Public Health Overview*. Summary of the Discipline of Public Health, Denver, Colorado (personal files of author).

Rutter, M. (1987, July). "Psychosocial Resilience and Protective Mechanisms", in *American Journal of Orthopsychiatry, 57*(3), pp.316-331.

United Nations Educational, Scientific and Cultural Organization. (2001). "The International Decade for a Culture of Peace and Non-Violence for the Children of the World (2001-2010)", in *Peace Is In Our Hands*. Retrieved 20/05/2004, from United Nations: http://www.unesco.org/iycp/uk_sum_decade/htm.

Vallejo Fighting Back Partnership, Inc. *Vallejo Neighbourhood Revitalization*. Retrieved 17/05/2004, from www.fightback.org/vnr.html.

World Council of Churches. (2001, 7/05). *Decade to Overcome Violence (2001-2010)*. Retrieved 20/05/2004, from World Council of Churches: http://www.wwc-coe.org/dov.

Chapter 2

Agosin, M. and Sepulveda, E. (2001). *Amigas: Letters of Friendship and Exile* (B. M. Morgan, Trans.). Austin TX, Univ. of Texas Press.

Bandura and Walters. (1965). *Social Learning and Personality Development*. New York, Holt Rinehart & Winston.

Bloom, S. and Reichert, M. (1998). *Bearing Witness: Violence and Collective Responsibility*. New York, Haworth.

Cohen, L. and Erlenborn, J. (1999). *Cultivating Peace in Salinas*. Salinas CA, Martella Printing.

Chute, T. (2001, 7/09). "Conflict Transformation for Teachers", in *Mennonite Central Committee News Service* (Guatemalan Mennonite Church).

Holsopple, M. Y. (2001, January). City of Salinas, *2000-2001 Annual Report, Peace and Justice Collaborative.* Elkhart IN.

Payne, R. K. (1995). *Poverty: A Framework for Understanding and Working with Students and Adults from Poverty.* Baytown TX, RFT Publishing.

United States Department of Health and Human Services. (2001). *Youth Violence: A Report of the Surgeon General.* Rockville MD, United States Department of Health and Human Services, Centres for Disease Control and Prevention, National Centre for Injury Prevention and Control; Substance Abuse and Mental Health Services Administration, Centre for Mental Health Services; and National Institutes of Health, National Institute of Mental Health.

Chapter 3

Harvard School of Public Health (1998). "Help from the Health Care Setting", In *Peace by Piece,* pp.125-133. Boston MA, Harvard School of Public Health Violence Prevention Programme.

Herman, J. (1997). *Trauma and Recovery.* New York, Basic Books.

Krug, E. G., Dahlberg, L. L., Mercy, J. A., Zwi and Lozano, R. (2002). *World Report on Violence and Health.* Geneva, World Health Organization.

Oklahoma State Department of Health. (2003). *Children First Programme.* Retrieved 11/21/03, from Oklahoma State Department of Health:
http://www.health.state.ok.us/programme/c1/index/html.

Remen, R. N. Retrieved 13/05/2004, from
http://www.commonweal.org/ishe/programmes/index.html.

Silver, S. M. (1986). "An Inpatient Programme for Post-Traumatic Stress Disorder: Context as Treatment", in C. R. Figley, ed., *Trauma and Its Wake.* New York, Brunner/Mazel.

Zehr, H. (2002). *The Little Book of Restorative Justice.* Intercourse PA, Good Books.

Chapter 4

Biggs, B. S. and Roddick, A. (2003). *Brave Hearts, Rebel Spirits: The Spiritual Activists' Handbook.* San Franscisco CA, Anita Roddick Publications.

Brock, R. N. and Parker, R. A. (2002), *Proverbs of Ashes.* Boston MA, Beacon.

Compassionate Listening Project. (1998). Retrieved 13/05/2004, from http://www.compassionatelistening.org.

Fellowship of Reconciliation. (2004). Retrieved 18/05/2004, from http://www.forusa.org.

Glide Memorial United Methodist Church. (established 1929). Glide. Retrieved 18/05/2004, from http://www.glide.org.

Recovery of Historical Memory Project. (1999). *Guatemala Never Again!* [Human Rights Office of the Archdiocese of Guatemala]. Maryknoll NY, Orbis.

Simpkinson, A. A. (2001). *Are We Ready to Forgive? Interview with Archbishop Desmond M. Tutu*. Retrieved 13/5/2004, from beliefnet: http://www.beliefnet.com/story/88/story_8880_1.html.

Tarbet, T. V. J. (2000). *Thomas Banyacya, Hopi Interpreter*. Retrieved 18/05/2004, from Thomas Banyacya, Interpreter: http://www.angelfire.com/on/GEAR2000/tbhopi.html.

Chapter 5

Bloom, S. and Reichert, M. (1998). *Bearing Witness: Violence and Collective Responsibility*. New York, Haworth.

Comstock, G. and Scharrer, E. (1999). *Television: What's On, Who's Watching, and What It Means*. San Diego CA, Academic Press.

Connolly, P., Smith, A. and Kelly, B. (2002). "Too Young to Notice?", in *University of Ulster Research Report*. Retrieved 09/05/2004, from http://www.community-relations.org.uk/about_the_council/press_releases/22/.

Grossman, D. (1998, 10/08). "Trained to Kill", in *Christianity Today*.

Harvard School of Public Health, Violence Prevention Programmes. (1998). *Peace by Piece*. Boston MA, Division of Public Health Practice, Harvard School of Public Health.

Indiana Tobacco Prevention and Cessation. (2002). *White Lies*. Retrieved 19/04/2004, from Pathway Productions: http://www.whitelies.tv.

Katz, J., & Earp, J. (1999). *Tough Guys: Violence, Media and the Crisis in Masculinity*. Video recording, dir. Jhally, Sut. North Hampton, MA: Media Education Foundation (82 mins).

Kilbourne, J. (2002). *Killing Us Softly3: Advertising's Image of Women*. Video recording, dir. Jhally, Sut. North Hampton MA, Media Education Foundation (34 mins).

Walsh, B. (2004, 1/6). *Television Changes Us* (article). Retrieved 01/06/2004, from University of Oregon-Eugene: http://interact.uoregon.edu.

Chapter 6

Cohen, B. (2003). *True Majority*. Retrieved 4/02/2003, from www.truemajority.com.

Cohen, L. and Erlenborn, J. (1999). *Cultivating Peace in Salinas: A Framework for Violence Prevention*. Salinas CA, Martella Printing.

Ford, A. and Mark, T. (2003, 2/9). "Self-Sufficiency Standard is a 'Bare Bones Budget' of What People Need", in *Elkhart Truth* (Elkhart IN), sec. Local News.

MacDonald, M. (1999). *All Souls: A Family Story from Southie*. Boston MA, Beacon.

Mattessich, P. W., Murrary-Close, M., Monsey, B. R. and Wilder Research Centre (2001). *Collaboration: What Makes It Work*. St. Paul MN, Amherst H. Wilder Foundation.

Moore, M. (Director). (2002). *Bowling for Columbine* (Film). Hollywood CA, Metro Goldwyn Mayer.

Chapter 7

God's Eye Art. (2000). *God's Eye Art*. Retrieved 19/05/2004, from God's Eye Art Inc.: http://www.godseyeart.com.

McNamara, C. (2002). "A Basic Guide to Programme Evaluation". Retrieved 19/05/2004, from *The Grantsmanship Center Magazine*. http://www.tgci.com/magazine/03fall/guide1.asp.

MADD. (2004). Mothers Against Drunk Driving. Retrieved 19/05/2004, from MADD National Office: http://www.madd.org/home/.

The Foundation Centre. (1995-2004). *Helping Grantseekers Succeed, Helping Grantmakers Make a Difference*. Retrieved 19/05/2004, from http://foundationcenter.org.

The Raging Grannies. (2004). *Songs We Sing*. Retrieved 19/05/2004, from http://www.geocities.com/raginggrannies/GrannySongs1.html.